Tantra Magick

Tantra Magick

The Manual of Tantra Magick Part I

(Modern Studies in Tantrik Magick Series Vol II)

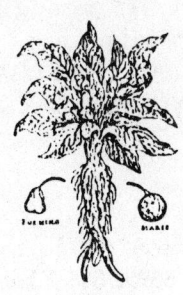

Mandrake

PO Box 250

Oxford OX1 1AP

Tantra Magick

Tantra Magick (c) AMOOKOS and Mandrake

All rights reserved. No part of this publication may be reproduced or transmitted in any form or by any means, electronic or mechanical, including photocopy, recording, or any other information storage and retrieval system, without permission in writing from the publisher.

Special Consultant: Shri Lokanath Maharaj

Printed in Great Britain by
Antony Rowe Ltd, Chippenham, Wiltshire

The authors and editors of this book have chosen to act anonymously. All royalties from sales will be donated by the publishers to the AMOOKOS Trust. This organisation is currently seeking charitable status and aims to protect and promote the interests of the AMOOKOS community. If you wish to make a donation or find out more write care of the publishers, enclosing return postage.

ISBN 1 86992 810 5 paperback
ISBN 1 86992 811 3 hardback

Summer Solstice 1990

Also in this Series
Michael Magee, *Tantrik Astrology* (Mandrake 1989)

Contents

Introduction
The Guru (7) The meaning of AMOOKOS (9) The AMOOKOS Charter (13).

Chapter One: The 1st degree: Apprentice
Symbolism of the Grade (15) Working the Grade (17) The Daily Rite (21) Study Topics (23) Symbolism of the Opening Rite (23) Astrology (26) Perception (27) Skrying (28) Shambhala (28) The Left Hand Path (29) The Siddhis (31)

Chapter Two: The 2nd degree: Esquire or Handmaiden
Symbolism of the Grade (37) Working the Grade (39) The Body Yantra (39) Sun-Moon-Fire Meditation (42) Ayurveda (42) Rite of Body Yantra (44) Amulet of the Great Goddess of Time (52) Mnemonics (52) The Kleshas (54) Academy of Symbolism (56) Academy of Five Senses (57) Maya (59) The Daily Rite (58) The word Natha

Chapter Three: The 3rd degree: Craftsman or Craftswoman
Symbolism of the Grade (63) The Rite of the Maha Zonule (65) Magick of the Five Elements (66) The Four twilights (70) Time Breath Science (71) Mantra (72) Yoginis of the Body Yantra (75) Paramashvari (78) Inner Magick of the Body Yantra (78) The Shri Yantra (79) Smashing the Five Kleshers (83) Astrological Theatre (84) Protection rite of Dattatreya (90) Ganesha (91) Dream Power (95) Siddhis: An Inner View (97) Time Lore (100) The Kaula Upanishad

Appendices
List of Symbols (115) Glossary of Terms (117) Index (122)

Tantra Magick

Introduction

The Guru

His Holiness Shri Gurudeva Mahendranath (Dadaji) was born in London in April 1911. From his early youth he had a deep interest in the occult and spiritual patterns of the world. In his early twenties he chanced to meet the infamous Aleister Crowley, whose hyperbole stirred and outraged Fleet Street in the twenties and thirties.

Crowley's advice to the young seeker was simple - go to the East to learn more of the occult and wisdom patterns which had flourished there from pre-Christian times. However, the Spanish Civil War - in which Dadaji fought against the Fascists as a member of the International Brigade - and the second world War intervened.

It was 1949 before Dadaji left the shores of Britain to arrive, penniless, in Bombay. There he was introduced by a mutual acquaintance to a sadhu of the Adinath cult. The Naths were at one time very numerous and influential in India; there are nine subsects, one of which is the Adinath cult. 'Nath', is Sanskrit for 'Lord' and is an epithet of Shiva, the Lord of Yoga. Initiates have names ending in 'nath'.

One of the Nath initiates - Goraknath - devised or reintroduced Hatha Yoga in the 11th Century. The Nath cult was also responsible for such works as the *Hatha Yoga Pradipika* and the *Shiva* and *Goraksha Samhitas*.

The sadhu introduced to Dadaji was the last remaining Adinath Yogi in all India, and was also the Adiguru or holder of the sacred line of tradition. Unlike some of the other sects of Naths the Adinath's chief interest was the Yoga of liberation from the restraining conditions of life, and to become free from the Wheel of *Samsara* or death and rebirth. Dadaji was initiated as a sannyasi by Adiguru Lokanatha, so becoming the first Englishman to become a sadhu.

A sadhu may make only three demands: for shelter - the shade of a tree; for clothing - rags. For food - leftover scraps. These conditions in former times helped the seeker after wisdom to realise the transitory and ultimately worthless nature of attachment.

In this the sadhus emulate the Guru figure of all India, Lord Dattatreya. Datta is the legendary founder and guardian spirit of many if not most of the Nath subsects. He represents a human being who has swung free of the three gunas or threads of Hindu philosophy from which the whole fabric of the Cosmos is said to be sewn. For this reason he is often pictured as a naked man with three heads and six arms to represent the Hindu Trinity of gods, Brahma, Vishnu and Shiva.

Tantra Magick

For the next thirty years Dadaji wandered South East Asia as a penniless sannyasi. His travels took him to Bhutan, where he was initiated into the Kargyupta Sect of Tibetan Lamaism. He also travelled to Malaysia where he became a Taoist priest and studied the I Ching, and to Ceylon, where he was for a time a Bhikku of Theravada Buddhism.

It may perhaps seem strange that a sannyasi of a Hindu tradition could also become a lama, a bhikku and a priest, but as many of the Eastern traditions recognize only sincerity in an aspirant for wisdom and knowledge there is no essential contradiction in a person having more than one guru or guide or seeking wherever an individual quest may lead.

During Dadaji's Indian wanderings, he met and was initiated by the last surviving Guru of the Uttara Kaulas of Northern Tantriks. He also became an initiate of the Naked Sahajiya cult of Benares.

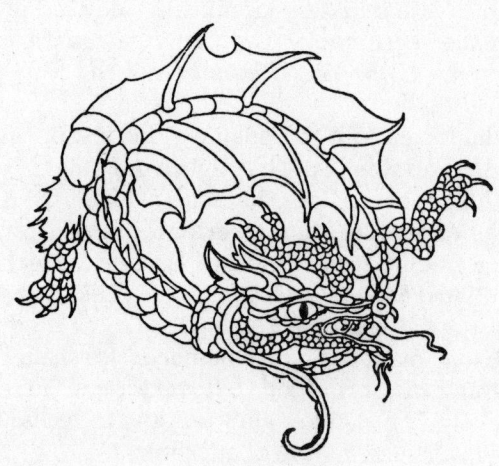

Introduction

AMOOKOS - The Arcane and Magickal Order of the Knights of Shambhala

In this book you will find the first three sets of instructions for the group AMOOKOS (the Arcane and Magickal Order of the Knights of Shambhala).

For the first time, we publicly reveal the methods, rites and philosophy pursued by an inner group of initiates within the Natha Community.

This book shows how the esoteric strands of east and west are fused together into a practical system which had as its purpose the unveiling of the spiritual potential latent in every individual. Initiates of AMOOKOS take as their starting point the assumption that within each and every human is a divine spark, the Alpha Ovule, or spirit, which simply had to be freed from the bonds or fetters of ignorance or conditioning to shine free.

As a presentation of practical methods for working towards self-knowledge, wisdom, and understanding, many may find the exercises in the different grade papers indispensable. Much of the material will not be found in any other tradition or teaching. Its rendering of the basics and essentials of tantrik practice in simple language is also new.

AMOOKOS was started at the behest of HH Shri Gurudeva Mahendranath. Wishing to transmit his own experience and the Nath transmission, in 1978 Mahendranath passed the parampara or line of transmission to a youthful 'seeker after truth'. At this point, the Adinath Sampradaya was transformed into an international group (See Charter below). Soon after, instructions were received to start a nine-grade group within the Naths, and AMOOKOS was the result.

Dadaji collaborated with the compilers of this material at every step, and approved their contents:

'the morning post arrived and another shake up with the grade two material. Astounding -- will take some days to get through it step by step.' 14 March 1983.

'I have been wandering again through AMOOKOS grade 1 and 2 material. It is stupendous, nectar of the wise. You have certainly produced a miracle explosion in the occult world.' 24 March 1983.

'The grade 3 papers are hyper-dimensional and this alone is a masterpiece of collated wisdom and expression.' 16 November 1983.

'AMOOKOS is a magical order for those who seek occult and magic power. Everything can be done through the post. Personal interviews are not essential."25 April 83.

Unlike many other esoteric schools, no pressure was put on initiates to pursue the material at any pace other than their own individual speed. At any time, without reason or explanation, a person could cease the work. The hierarchical structure which had condemned many other groups to political intrigues and power struggles never affected AMOOKOS.

In the few years since it was founded, not one person was expelled from the Order. Zonules or Lodges of the group rapidly took root in the United States, in Sweden, in West Germany, in the UK, in Spain, and even in the Philippines. The first zonule was started in London, so fulfilling the prediction contained in the Meru Tantra (17th century) which stated that tantriks would practise in London who would use an English language mantra and would become lords of the world.

At its best, the structure of AMOOKOS acts in the same way as a training course. The names and paraphernalia surrounding each of the grades were never regarded seriously by initiates of the Order. What does matter was that practical work is done. No one ever had any doubt that the grade structure was more than a convenient fiction.

The Golden Dawn had made the mistake of correlating its grade structure with the qabalistic Tree of Life, so that initiates were led into thinking that the higher their grade, the closer they were to the 'top of the tree'. In fact, the Middle Group of AMOOKOS knew that their task was to become independent, free from all names and forms. Why substitute one rat-race for another?

In this, they followed the precepts of *Svecchachara*, a Sanskrit compound which means the path of following one's own true will (Sva = own, Iccha = will, Achara = path). If the work of the AMOOKOS grades was successful, an individual would finally realise that the grades and work were simply a means to an end, to be discarded once the essence was extracted. Because most candidates started as conditioned beings, the gradual stripping of these layers or fetters would allow what had always been there to be fully expressed. Any method leading to this true self was useful. Names such as Nath, and groups such as AMOOKOS, could only remain as relative things. When spirit is free, what matter the name its outer form is given? The rigmarole and ritualism of the first three grade papers were regarded by adepts of the group as the fuel to fire self-knowledge.

The course-work contained within this book, while expressed simply enough, is a rigorous regime of practical yogic work. The

Introduction

aspirant is led from simple beginnings to more and more complex exercises and visualisations, the final aim being freedom from the conditioning and brainwashing all experience in this life.

An example of what is demanded of AMOOKOS initiates is shown by the second Grade Paper The five Academies of Sense Perception. This is an exercise in awareness spanning a period of six months, and involving the initiate in a re-assessment of how she or he sees the world. Initiates regarded this as a key exercise. It certainly isn't easy to achieve. While most people think they use their five senses, this exercise showed them just how little they did use. Because of the substitution of labels (words) for direct experience, the different gradations of colour, smell, taste, touch, and hearing are lost when people are quite young.

Tantra Magick contains the Grade Papers of the preliminary level of the Western Nath Order AMOOKOS.

The word Nath implies the AMOOKOS member's main aim: to realise herself or himself as a master - the meaning of the word Natha.

One major key is access to the Kala Chakra patterns, which allow for an objective and extensive investigation into any time bound thing. Another key is knowledge of inner and subtle physiology, which allows the potential of the various centres to be realised, and balances a human being.

The third key is the inner tradition of freedom and tolerance common to the Nath traditions, and the development of spontaneity, perfect assimilation, and equipoise.

Initiation implied no acceptance of exoteric or cultural elements peculiar to India. The same fountain that inspired the Naths also flowed westward, northwards to Tibet, eastwards to China and Japan, and south to India and Sri Lanka. So any cultural elements attached to the inner tradition are completely superfluous.

AMOOKOS is subdivided into 3 groups: Outer, Middle, and Inner Temple. These aligned with ancient tantrik classification into Pashu (herd), Vira (heroines and heroes), and Divya (spiritually attained). The first three degrees were training degrees. Initiates are encouraged to work practically -- the first practical work for any esotericist being deconditioning.

The work helps to introduce students to basic concepts of both eastern and western spiritual work. The grades are not hierarchical, but similar to levels in a school. Advancement is solely on the basis of completion of each successive stage.

In the Middle Temple, initiates are given the opportunity to found their own zonules, encampments or lodges. Spiritual work became of a more independent nature. Zonule holders have autonomy in the running of their own encampment. AMOOKOS wanted to encourage independence for people, and so avoid the problems of egotism, factionalism, and 'grade congestion' -- problems which have plagued many Western groups.

The Inner Temple was for people who wish to pursue their own spiritual path, and who need no props, guidance or instruction from others.

Membership is open to any sincere person of 18 years or more. There are no financial obligations. There was an obligation not to communicate grade material to non-initiates. Members are free to leave AMOOKOS at any time, and for any reason, or, if they choose, to suspend their work for resumption at a later date.

Many will wish to know the reason why these instructions are now being made more generally available. The major and important reason is that as the world approaches the millenium, members of the Natha Community feel that all should be able to take advantage of the exercises and wisdom contained in these papers. At the same time, the corruption, back-biting and factionalism of different esoteric groups is a scandal to those who seek a spiritual path. Individual zonule holders throughout the world are continuing their work of guidance, experimentation and study.

The international Nath Community wishes to make available its methods and philosophy to all. The time for secret hole-in-the-wall groups is over.

Charter of AMOOKOS

Be it known that on this New Year Day, January the First, Nineteen Hundred and Seventy-Eight, this decision, being my true Will and Wish has been put into immediate operation.

Therefore I, Shri Gurudeva Dadaji Mahendranath, the only surviving Supreme Guru of the Adi Natha Sampradaya - the Cult and Organization of the First and Supreme Sacred Lords of the Spiritual Cosmos; King of Shambhala and Grand Lord of its Knights; Keeper of the Firth Book of the Nine Secret Chiefs, Merlin of Cockaigne and Light of the Silver Star; do hereby ordain by that Supreme Authority which rests with me, that the Adi-Nath Sampradaya shall from henceforth become an International and Cosmopolitan Order of all Worthy People, students and householders above the age of eighteen years, who may occupy a normal life and pursuit of livelihood; provided always that they accept the three basic aims and objects of the Nathas - to wit - real Peace, Real Freedom and Real Happiness. Therefore from the Naked Guru to Naked Sishya, the Transmission and Initiation shall be given to all Noble Masters, Magicians, Alchemists, Masons, Rosicrucians, Astrologers and Occultists of stable nature who will bond themselves into one Grand Concord of Cosmic People and Work, Experiment and Teach for the weal and welfare of all mankind. This new promulgation does not prevent or discourage those whom as Nathas wish to become Hermits, Sannyasins, Anchorites or Recluses if they wish to do so. To finalize this decision of a greater and more expansive Order, the Initiation and Parampara (line of Nath succession) has now been passed on by me to Shri Lokanath Maharaj, Lord of Cockaigne and Prince of Babalon that He may continue the line of succession and pass it on to all other worthy people. This is our law, the Rhythm of the Cosmos by which the Wise must live.

Chapter One: The Apprentice
(AMOOKOS Grade Paper 1)

Introduction
To start work in AMOOKOS you will first have to assemble those things required to work the grade. It will be necessary for you to resolve to actually do the work - our path is a practical one, and the higher realms cannot be introduced all at once.

The papers of the first degree are designed to be useful for both beginners and people who have had some experience of the esoteric. The work included is designed to give members a foundation for the more demanding work which follows.

You should take your time with the grade and not be in too much of a hurry. Read the chapter through once to familiarise yourself with its contents. Assemble whatever is necessary.

Make daily efforts with perception (page 27) and the Daily Rite (pages 21 to 22).

Make weekly experiments in your laboratory zonule with skrying (page 28). At your leisure, familiarise yourself with the system of mnemonics, and with the symbolism on page 23 if it is unfamiliar to you. Study and reflect on the rest of your material at your Will.

Symbolism of the Grade
Symbol:
Measuring stick. We can see three aspects to this: the Measure, the Measurer and the Measured. An object, that which may be measured, may only be known by the measurer (subject) through an instrument or measuring-stick. One of our first tasks is to make a valid instrument by which the whole Cosmos may be measured.
This ruler is divided into 5 sections. More will be learnt of this in the Academy of the 5 senses, while working the second grade.

Colour:
Emerald Green. You may use cloth of this colour to sit on when meditating in the place of the Dragon-Seat, in the Umbra Zonule.

Gem:
Green stone, such as an emerald. This may be incorporated into a ring or other jewellery for use in a Lodge.

Tantra Magick

Work:
implies the assembly by you of all the elements and artefacts required to work this grade.

Necklace:
Simple bead

Number of units:
3

Zonule name:
Assembly

Animal:
Cat

Place of meeting:
Rooms

> *The Sage Kings have ordained*
> *All members should understand:*
> *The secrets of our life are found in the oracle and the divine has inscribed them on the skin of the tiger; but the lines are very coarse.*
> *The secrets of the lord of light are seen in the cosmos and on leaves, the bark of trees, in strong vines and leather thongs. They are recorded most delicately on the skin of the noble Panther.*
> *The mysteries of the masters are seen on high mountains and recorded on rocks and stones, and in flames of fire, and in winding rivers.*
> *The patterns for churls are found in the forests and recorded on leaves, the bark of trees, in strong vines and leather thongs.*
> *The Sage Kings have given that the secrets of humankind will be found in the inner nature, and revealed on the placid lake of tranquility.*
> *There is a power of light and a power of darkness, and we must learn to discriminate; never become enmeshed in evil hopes or dark aims.*
> *If you see life in tiny pieces, the world in sections, and think only in minute particles and divisions, then report to the High Executioner.*

The Apprentice

Working The Grade

The Diary

From the very beginning, keep a record of your experiments and work. In it you should write the date, the practice, and any impressions, memories or feelings that may arise. Strive to write accurately and freely, and keep the diary up to date.

Its cover and its interior may be adorned with any symbols, patterns of colours that you feel express your aspirations. No-one in the order will ask to see your diary, although you are free to discuss it with your co-members if you desire. The size of the book is entirely up to you, although from practical experience we advise it be no smaller than A5, with a hard cover.

Umbra Zonule

The work of members of AMOOKOS takes place in the *Umbra Zonule* (literally: twilight circle). This is the place where magickal energy is raised, directed or absorbed. All individual and group work takes place in this area. Trace a circle about yourself. You may use chalk, or coloured powders, or the circle may also be visualised or traced with the point of a wand. The centre of the zonule is called the Dragon-Seat.

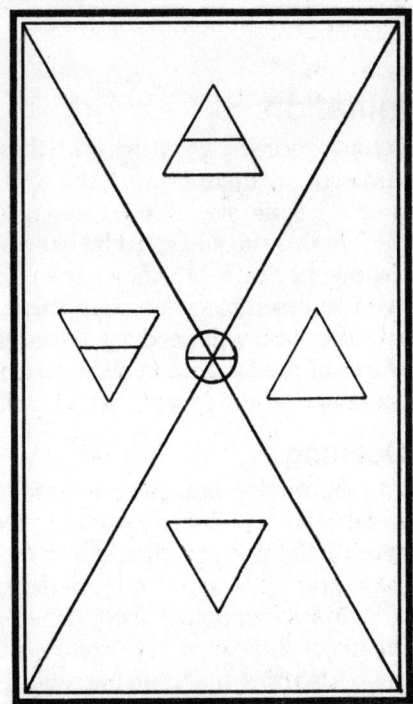

You should assemble the following in order to represent the five elements:

Aether:
The Will of the Magician [a red pentagram]
Air:
An incense stick is its symbol
Fire:
A brazier, candle, or oil lamp
Water:
Water in a bowl
Earth:
Foodstuff

These should be placed in the appropriate quarters as shown in the diagram.

Tantra Magick

Rites should not be performed in the direction wherein falls the first letter of the place-name of the location of the rite. This injunction applies to particular rather than general rituals.

The place of Aether is the Dragon-Seat. Prepare the zonule daily, and spend a period of time in meditation. Have your diary near you - in it you may record any impressions you have. Do not be hasty. Relax, assume a comfortable position. If the temperature permits it is better to be naked, but your own preference is the best guide.

The best times for work in the UZ are twilight times - dawn and dusk. However, any time is good; in this matter there are no fixed and hard rules. We include on page 21 a ritual which you should perform each day.

Initiation

Before proceeding to work with these papers, it is essential that you are initiated. If there is no local AMOOKOS group (Zonule) then you should do this at a time prearranged time with your magickal Guide.

In this rite you must be naked. Beforehand you should have had a shower or bath. Do not wear any jewellery on this occasion. You will need to assemble your equipment to represent the elements and in addition, you will need ash in order to consecrate your body with the marks of the Tantrik. In order to close the Zonule you will also need a container of some sort in which you can light a small fire.

Opening

You should open a Zonule in the following manner: Make a circle of any suitable size and by any suitable means. Whether within a dwelling or beneath the sky, you should be naked and apart from the initiation you may wear ornaments and jewellery if desired.

Mark four points around the circumference of the circle to indicate the major directions. The centre is the Dragon Seat.

Also present within the circle should be flame, incense, fruit, water

The Apprentice

and a red pentagram. The first four should be placed in the quarters, the last directly in front of you.

Face the east, and dispense with any negative energies by snapping the fingers of the right hand or making some other sharp noise - such as the Vajra Mantra *PHAT*. Do the same in the order East, South, West, North, South-East, South-West, North-West, North-East, Above and Below.

Facing East, and being seated, say:
I salute the line of innumerable Naths
And cast the Circle of Dragon Glow
May my Zonule be intact
And the peace of Om Shiva Shakti dwell herein.

Clap the hands together, three times, loudly. Place the hands upon the respective parts of the body, saying:
I salute Shiva Shakti in my heart
I salute Shiva Shakti on the crown of my head
I salute Shiva Shakti on the top of my forehead
I salute Shiva Shakti in my armour [1]
I salute Shiva Shakti in my three eyes
I salute Shiva Shakti in my yoni/linga

Take three deep breaths. At the end of each breath, say:
Om, Peace-Freedom-Happiness to all the Members of Amookos
Om, I salute the Triple Natured Goddess
Om, I salute the Lord of Awareness

Now visualise the four guardians of the directions:

Still facing East, bow, and visualise the form of a naked young goddess, with skin the colour of beaten gold, in sexual union with a man.

Turning to the South, bow, and visualise the form of a naked young goddess, red in colour, with flaming eyes, who sits astride a scarlet lion.

Turning to the West, bow, and visualise the form of a naked young goddess, blue in colour, glistening with moisture, with beautiful large eyes, who bestraddles a noble eagle.

Turning to the North, bow, visualising a naked young goddess with a peaceful smiling face, of a green colour, seated on the back of a bull.

Face East again.

Tantra Magick

The Initiation Rite

After sitting quietly for about five minutes, you should light incense and flame, pour water, and assemble the symbols of the elements in their appropriate quarters.

Visualise that you, in the UZ, are surrounded by a cone of intense white light, and that at the point of this cone is a vortex of energy. Imagine that the light of Shambhala [2] enters through the crown of your head, flooding firstly brain, then heart, then genitals.

Visualise the region of your brain as the Moon, your heart as the Sun, and your genitals as Fire. Meditate: my thoughts are reflective, my heart is steady and warm, fire is my passion...for some few minutes. You should then stand and say:

Nakedness shall be my symbol of freedom
A symbol of my new birth into the Magick Life
It is the highest expression of Creation
Through the mind and body of every human being
Through the intellect, feelings and sense expressions
The Creator enjoys the world and cosmos thus created
I seek sincerely to study the occult sciences
I seek to know more of the magickal way of life
I renounce shame, shyness and inhibitions
I renounce the ways of darkness and ignorance

Now mark the 8 appropriate parts of your body with ash:

I consecrate my brow to Divine Wisdom
I consecrate my breasts to love's embrace
I consecrate my genitals to the Creator's enjoyment
I consecrate my hands to eternal service
I consecrate my feet to walk our path
The rite is complete
I salute the triple-natured Goddess
I salute the Lord of awareness
Peace-freedom-happiness to all members of AMOOKOS

Realise yourself to be born into a new existence as the Lady or Knight of Shambhala, and once again sit quietly and meditate for a few moments.

Closing

To close this, or any similar rite, turn to the NE, where resides a Goddess dressed all in red, holding in her hands a skull cup and a pair of scissors, seated on a corpse. Here you should have placed previously a container of some sort in which a small fire may be burnt. Be careful! After eating any remaining fruit and having drunk any water, the remains of your

The Apprentice

ritual accessories should be placed in this container, and burnt as an offering to this Goddess, Shoshita, whose function it is to consume leftovers.

Face East once more, visualise the four Goddesses of the Quarters merging into you, sit for a while in meditation, and say,

I close my Umbra Zonule
May all experience peace, freedom and happiness!
Om Shiva Shakti!

The Daily Rite

Opening

Open your Umbra Zonule by performing the Opening Rite (part one of the initiation ritual).

The Pentagram Rite

While seated within your Umbra Zonule proceed with the Pentagram Rite. Place five small vessels at each point of your Pentagram. Offer incense, flame, water and food to each of the five Goddesses at the five points (see diagram). As you do so, meditate upon their forms saying:

Fragrant maiden goddess of sweet-smell, I bow to your beautiful arrow-form. May I be awake and alert!

Sweet Smell: She is young and beautiful, garlanded with white flowers and is naked, save for her silver ornaments. Her hair is arranged in a lovely way.

Sweet honey-eyed lady of the truth of touch, I bow to your beautiful arrow form. May my being awake!

Touch Truth: She is young and beautiful, garlanded with green, save for the many emeralds which stud her anklets, necklace and rings. She stands, soft-footed, in a beautiful grassy meadow, surrounded by lovely hills.

Scented and true-hearted maiden of taste, I bow to your beautiful arrow form. Let me always taste!

Taste Maiden: Her true heart shows through her beautiful eyes, and she is in the first bloom of youth, wearing only sapphire ornaments. Food and drink are at her feet.

Garlanded girl of hearing, I bow to your beautiful arrow form. May I awake to reality!

Girl of hearing: She wears gold ornaments. She is bright eyed, playing softly on a stringed instruments. She is surrounded by trees, each one full of sweetly singing birds which are in harmony with her music. She sits by a murmuring stream, and in her immediate backgrounds is a snow peaked mountain.

Naked flower-girl, lovely lady of sight, I bow to your beautiful arrow form. May I always see clearly!

Sight Arrow: Her beautiful naked form is smeared with red paste. Seven rainbows seem to end at her feet. Peacocks in full display walk by her. The sun is high in the sky.

Now imagine, or visualise, that each of these maidens merges into one Goddess, in the centre, who is their unity.

Arrow Goddess of the Five: She is as red as the dawn, naked (clothed in space), her body drenched with the sweet nectar of ecstasy, she holds in her two hands five arrows and five flowers. She smiles gently, and is satisfied and contented.

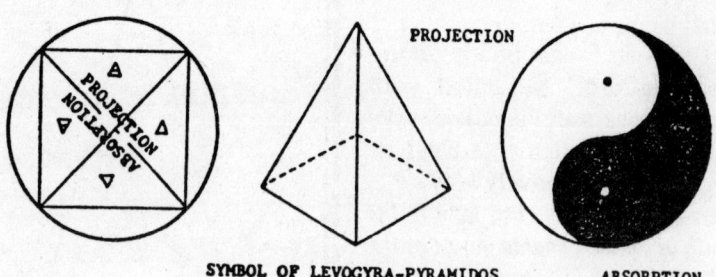

SYMBOL OF LEVOGYRA-PYRAMIDOS

The Apprentice

Study topics
You will need an Ephemeris to cover the next year. See also details of further reading, at the end of this chapter.

The Opening Rite - an introduction to its symbolism

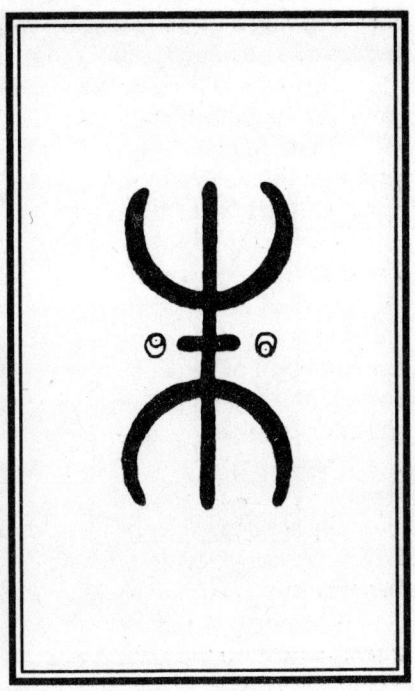

The first degree of AMOOKOS can be viewed symbolically as the first Temple, City, or Gate on our Kaula island of Amookos-Shambhala. We discuss the term Shambhala more fully below, on page 28. In AMOOKOS we see this land of peace, freedom and happiness as an internal place, located within our own bodies. Amookos-Shambhala has nine enclosures in all, each a pleasure-garden of delight.

For the new member, the ramparts of this city are guarded on their four sides by four celestial yoginis (female yogis), or goddesses, each mounted on their magical beasts.

At the centre of the city-complex of Shambhala is a Meru-Lingam, Merlin or Staff which supports the world. Here is Adinath Shiva with his Shakti. Adinath is a Sanskrit word which means the Primordial Lord. The Kaula Island itself is in the centre of an ocean of nectar or ambrosia.

All this is symbolically resumed in the grade papers by the body yantra. A yantra is simply the representation, in the form of a diagram, of a spiritual truth. They frequently offer many interpretations. For instance, the body yantra is an emblem both of the body itself, and of the two luminaries, sun and moon, and the earth. The Dragon Seat of the Umbra Zonule is the Bindu or centre of the circle. But this is also identical with the meru lingam in the symbolism of the island of Amookos. You will come to study the Body Yantra in depth while working the second grade.

The Dragon Lords or Secret Chiefs of Amookos each hold the double trident or Vajra [3] which signifies the human body - two arms,

two legs, head and genitals. You will see that this is also the Sun and Moon in one figure, or above-below. [4]

The beasts which guard the ramparts of the Island of AMOOKOS are animal forms of Shiva, and the yoginis or Goddesses are forms of Shakti, or the Goddess Kalika, who is the Lady of Time.

You can represent these in the UZ as crystal, ruby, sapphire and emerald lingas or penises set in golden yonis or vaginas. If represented in this way, a red trident should be marked on the lingam.

More esoterically, the four forms represent the angles or corners of an Amookos time-breath chart, or breath-cycle, known vulgarly as a horoscope. East is the Ascendent, South is the Midheaven, West is the Descendant, and North is the Lower Heaven. These four together make one day of Shambhala.

Such a day is not reckoned in hours but in minutes and equals 24 hours x 60 minutes = 1440 minutes. (In the Lunar Kalendar there are 15 days or Eternities, that is to say 21600 minutes.)

Each of the four lokapalas - that is, pairs of World Protectors or guardians - is, therefore, 360 minutes (a quarter of a day) and each pair also forms in itself a complete cycle or circle (360 degrees). You may call each pair what you will so long as it be remembered they are a pair: Shiva-Shakti. We call them Dawn, Midday, Sunset and Midnight, or the four Twilights. In each pair there is light and darkness, yin and yang.

These four twilights occur in one Shambhala day, and also in a year of Shambhala. There are four festivals to mark these four twilights. These occur at the two Equinoxes and two solstices: Spring =Dawn, Summer = Midday, Autumn = Sunset, Winter = Midnight.

The diagram overleaf - shows the interplay between light and dark.

The Amookos Adinath tradition states that magickal acts and rites performed at the twilights are the most efficacious. In the Indian

The Apprentice

subcontinent the twilights are said to be the times when Lord Shiva rules the earth.

The symbols of the four Twilights should be represented in every Zonule or UZ of AMOOKOS. You should attempt to draw them for yourself, or alternatively may visualise the yoni-lingas as described above.

In your own body the four twilights are represented by the groups Cerebral (△) Genital (△) Oral (▽) and Anal (▽). It should be noted these are grouped into two pairs - Cerebral/Genital and Oral/Anal. The former rests on the nervous system, the latter on the alimentary canal.

When taken together, the four Guardians or Lokapalas make up a Sphynx, or riddle of Egypt. In the breath-cycle astrology of Amookos, the four angles are exceedingly important. The Angles represent the planet earth, and the secret centre of that, in Shambhala, is the Wizardess or Wizard who sits in the centre of the UZ on the Dragon Seat.

Shambhala can be seen as a pyramid, its four sides of Shambhala-Pyramidos representing the four elements. The summit of the Pyramid has a similar significance to the peak of Mount Shambhala or the centre, Meru-Lingam - if the four conditions are met and are in balance then it

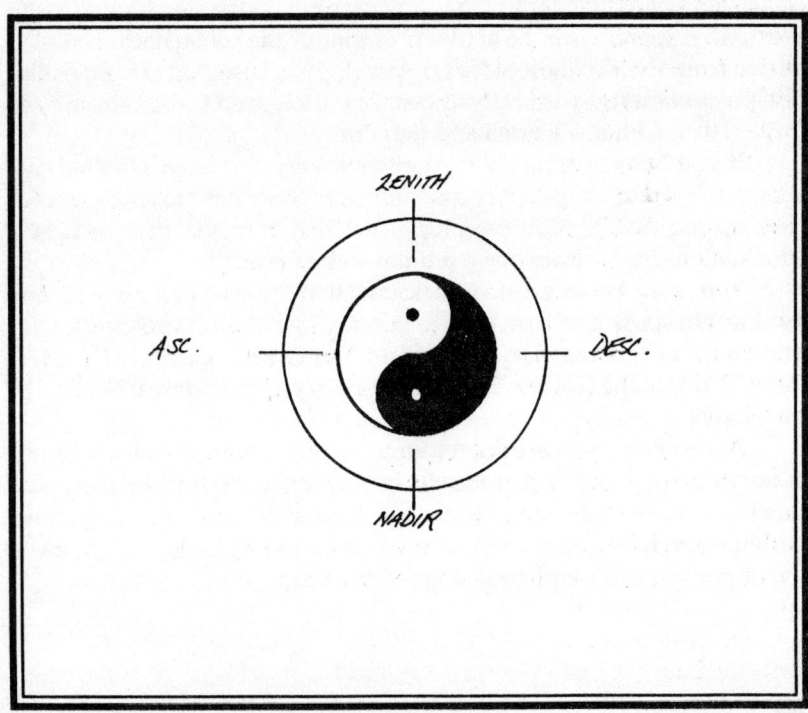

may be said to exist.

A word about Shiva and Shakti. Shiva is the primordial god and Shakti the primordial goddess. Although there are many different names of the God and the Goddess, we Kaulanaths hold that they are simply adjectives of the primordial God and Goddess. As the Naths followed Nature, so the most natural thing was to visualise the Creator as a female-male union - after all this is how creation takes place on earth.

Astrology

The art of astrology is an essential adjunct to our work. From determining good times for the performance of rites, knowing the position of the Moon, and for understanding one's own psychology, astrology will prove very useful to you.

It is necessary to distinguish between Tropical and Sidereal astrology. The former enjoys a vogue in the West, and its history is confused. It is based on the Spring Equinox coinciding with 0 degree Aries. In reality, because of the phenomenon known as the precession of the equinoxes, the Spring Equinox has not coincided with the stars of the constellation Aries since the 5th Century AD.

This means that none of the zodiacal signs, as they are known in the West, correspond with the actual positions of the constellations which derive from their names. Sidereal Astrology is based on the constellation positions as they actually appear in the sky, and is the astrology of India, Tibet, China, Chaldea and Babylon.

If you have previously studied astrology and been satisfied, we would ask you to temporarily suspend your beliefs and to take a careful look at our AMOOKOS astrology, the real function of which is a spiritual one, to become free from the web of rebirth.

You may be interested to know that Pythagoras, one of our 'brothers in spirit' is still revered to this day by Hindu Astrologers, who know him as Yavanacharya (Sanskrit: The Greek Teacher). The Hermetic Order of the Golden Dawn also promoted the sidereal version of astrology.

At this stage, you are not required to make a comprehensive study of the principles, but will gradually be introduced to further aspects of this work. In the meantime, try to learn the symbols of astrology, and perhaps purchase a current Ephemeris - such as Raphaels' - which gives the important cosmic phenomena for one year.

The Apprentice

Mnemonics

The first goal of a member of Amookos must be to free herself or himself from conditioning, and to think independently. On this all else depends.

Much you will find here is not usually classed as 'occult' but proficiency in the methods will be an invaluable aid to visualisation and imagination, essential skills, and also give you an insight into the subscience called Association of Thought. Aside from any of these considerations, you will find Mnemonics useful in everyday life.

Compile a list of words which rhyme with the numbers:

1-10, eg 1 Bun, 2 Shoe, 3 Tree, etc. Keep the rhymes simple. When you have made or memorised the list you are ready to proceed. Ask someone to read you a list of ten objects she or he has thought of. As you hear the words, associate each with the words you have linked to the numbers, for instance, Apple Bun 1, Car Shoe 2, etc.

As you hear the words read out, make an image which links the two words. For example, a bun with applesauce, a car in the shape of a shoe. Making these associations, you will be able to remember in any sequence, the list of words read out. Test the person who doesn't know this method by reading out ten words and seeing if they can repeat them in any sequence.

The second method involves linking each word of a list with the next word, creating a chain. For example: apple/car (a car in the shape of an apple); car/dog (a dog with wheels) etc.

Practise these methods until you are proficient. One objection often raised is that these methods seem time-consuming and elaborate. If you try the test of remembering ten words without using either method you will see how helpless you are without them.

Further material of greater practical use has been prepared, but first become proficient in both of the above methods.

Perception

As you may have intuited from the Pentagram Rite, perceptual awareness is an essential adjunct to our work. One may go very far using only these methods. The curriculum of the five Academies of perception commences in the second Grade.

The object of this work is not merely to increase the range of the sense organs themselves, but to increase the quality of awareness. To change the perception from passive to active.

In ordinary development word-association prevents the senses from functioning actively at an early stage in life. All results are to be entered in your diary.

Tantra Magick

Skrying

The development, in positive ways, of the imaginative faculties will aid your work in many ways. A useful aid to the development of psychic and other faculties is Skrying, whether in a crystal or a darkened glass.

A crystal is expensive but the following is a cheap alternative. Take a wine goblet, and coat its inside with the soot from a candle. Take care not to crack the glass by applying too much heat. A glass of black ink could also be used.

Before attempting to skry, open the UZ in the appropriate manner, and sit quietly gazing into the glass. Do not concentrate over much, but rather let the mind flow freely. Observe any images that may arise, and note them afterwards in your diary. You may try this experiment once a week.

Shambhala

Shambhala is a Sanskrit word, occuring in many Hindu texts. It even appears in dictionaries of the Sanskrit language, giving it the meaning of "wanton woman", and a town in Uttar Pradesh. This town still exists, and it is the place where Kalki, the tenth Avatar of Vishnu, and identical with Rudrachakrin, is to be reborn at some future time.

In *Bhagavata Purana* (ancient legends of the Divine), reference is made to Shambhala in this sense. The appearance on earth of the Spirit of Lord Kalki (Kalkinath) marks the period known as *Satya Yuga*, the Aeon of Truth, the Golden Age in the past. This age closes the dark age of Kali yuga.

When the dark age has passed its nadir, and reached a stage of exhaustion (marked by terror, intrigue, domination and chaos), the spirit of the Divine is to manifest in Shambhala as Lord Kalki. He is associated with two symbols, that of the flaming sword and the white horse.

Flaming sword may also be expressed as a sword of flame, as it does not mean sword in an aggressive sense, but a flame shaped like a sword. In detail, this flame means a new dispensation, a new Way of Life, new and different values which are to bring light to people who have endured in darkness. The sword implies destruction as the new will destroy the old way's systems and ideas.

The white horse is important because this animal is not an indigenous animal to India. It came originally from the lands North, East and West of the Himalayas. It therefore indicates something foreign, or from outside India. A new way of life cannot be a continuity of something old.

All of the foregoing has a deeper meaning than might be expected.

The Apprentice

We do not interpet Kalki as an actual person to incarnate on earth, but rather a symbol of something, some inner impulse which has to flower within us.

The dark age represents conditioned being, the spirit of Kalki the Light which is the light of spirit. Not being dependent on the old or ancient, the only weapon to achieve this internal New Aeon is that of truth.

Many books have suggested an actual Shambhala exists or existed, a place where everything was sweetness and light. We have to reject this. If this country of peace, freedom and happiness is to exist, then it must be an internal place. For these reasons we come across Shambhala as being located at various points within the human body.

In Amookos we sometimes call ourselves Shambhala International, because any place which is a meeting point for Kaula Naths may be said to be a Shambhala - but only if we are courageous and open enough to embrace truth.

Shambhala and the Left Hand Path (Vama Marg)

If we investigate the differences between an esoteric (left hand) and an exoteric (right hand) path, we can construct a comparative chart:

Shambhala	Agharti
Left hand path	Right hand path
Hard to grasp	Easy to grasp
Tantrik	Orthodoxy
Science	Superstition
Meditation	Priestcraft/prayer

'Left hand path' in India has not the same derogatory connotation as in the West. It means the path where sexuality and death are taken into account, where being individual is important, where there are no rules. Right hand paths lay down rules for the orthodox to follow - no effort is required according to the priests; just follow the instructions and you will go to heaven.

It is necessary to mention here that due to its antinomian tendency, the Shambhala path suffers greatly at the hands of uninitiated writers. Attempts have been made to lay all the crimes of mankind at the hands of the Tantriks, people whose only crime was not to try and change others. In Amookos we have a saying: Don't try and change the world, just make sure it doesn't change you.

In the right hand paths the weeds of politics and priestcraft flourish - it is the land of easy answers, rationalizations, control of the masses, "God is on our side", and labels for everything.

Meditation

Few are born with the ability to practice the different esoteric patterns and most need to develop and formulate them through meditation.

This is a most practical means by which we may know and recall that which has never really been lost, the identity of ourselves with the Divine.

There can never be an universal meditation system for all people. Most do best when they settle for their own individual patterns. Guidance only can be given. Only begin when you know what you want to do.

Enter the UZ, sit cross-legged, comfortable and relaxed. No props are needed, nor elaborate postures. Keep awake, or you will have entered the realm of failure. Trance, unconsciousness and sleep are instruments of defeat.

In the preliminary and early exploratory mind wanderings, concentrate by counting the breaths. Count the breath as it moves in and out, one to seven, repeat. Breath is synonymous in Amookos with the Divine. We have words in our language which express this - atmosphere of Greek origin has the same root as atman of Sanskrit, meaning spirit, or breath.

It should be clear that it is not necessary to meditate 'on' anything. It is enough in the early stages to just observe the processions of trains-of-thought. It is not the aim of meditation practice to obliterate thought. This would be impossible. The aim of meditation is to disentangle the observer, the measurer from the sea of thoughts in which she or he is normally entangled.

By observing the chains, many hints as to one's own word-web may be discovered. These often have emotional bases, and can form the seed or nucleus of obstacles, conditioning and dark thoughts.

Be sure to record carefully in your diary the results of your work.

The Siddhis - Psychic Realms

This paper covers a wide variety of subjects in brief form. It is not claimed for this paper that it is a comprehensive guide to the different topics. Members of AMOOKOS are encouraged to explore these subjects for themselves according to their interests.

The Apprentice

It has been our experience in twenty-four years of study that accomplishment in these *siddhis* (magickal powers) is very much rarer than one would think from the vast amount of literature relating to them. Many people claim expertise but the student should beware of taking such claims on face value.

The AMOOKOS standpoint is that some people seem to be born with a share of these siddhis, but conditioning and mind-fog obscures them. If an active spiritual disposition arises in an individual then the siddhis arise naturally. There seems to be an inbuilt protection against their full development in someone not pursuing a spiritual path. This is not to say that everyone claiming such powers are frauds, there are people who either genuinely believe they possess such powers or else actually do possess them to some extent. The AMOOKOS member should cultivate an open mind tempered with a healthy scepticism.

A times in local Zonules groups may experiment with these techniques in a practical fashion.

Psychometry

This is the ability to pick up information psychically from objects. This is sometimes extended to include photographs or pictures of people or places. Every object is said to somehow 'soak up' psychic emanations. If such an object has been in close proximity with an individual it may have a field surrounding it or permeating it which reflects that of its owner.

As a guide to practice our advice would always be to set up your UZ before experimenting. Take the object and hold it lightly. Allow your mind to relax, and observe any images or words which may arise. It is important to aid rejecting information, and for this reason it seems to be important to say the first thing which occurs to you, however ludicrous or ridiculous it may seem.

Astral Travel

This is a very popular subject, and there are many books relating to it. However it is important to be sure that you have the same understanding of the term as the author. What is called out of the body experience or Astral Travel by psychics and experimenters is often confused with the process of creative imagination practised by the Golden Dawn and other modern western magickal orders.

We talk here about Out Of the Body Experience related to what psychics often term the 'etheric' body. This is considered by many to be a similacrum of the physical body existing in a subtle form, and attached to the physical body by a subtle cord. There are many techniques related to this practice. Sometimes separation of the 'etheric' from the physical body occurs spontaneously. This is discussed further in chapter three.

Everyone's experience seems to differ slightly. It is possible to train in the various techniques to accomplish separation. However it is often easier to travel by British Airways than to accomplish it.

Clairvoyance and Clairaudience

These words imply the ability to 'see' or hear psychically. There are spiritists who claim the ability to see spirit guides and souls. Once again discrimination should be employed. Use your own standards to judge validity.

Magickal Links and Psychic Attack

A psychic link between an object and an individual (as in psychometry) can be used for magickal purposes - according to shamans and wizards of past and present. For this reason such things as nail clippings, hair and bodily secretions have always been regarded as things which should be carefully disposed of. Paranoia creeps in here. Remember that a person calling herself or himself a wizard or a witch does not mean she or he is one.

In our experience genuine 'psychic attack' is an exceedingly rare phenomenon. If on the other hand, you take it upon yourself to attempt such an attack upon another, remember that in AMOOKOS such a course may only be taken after consulting two other Yogi-Magicians of the Middle Temple. It is very rare for such an attempt to be warranted - look to yourself for the muddy reasons behind your motives of dark and revenge.

As far as initiates of AMOOKOS go there is no reason for anyone to fear 'psychic attack' by others. Our line is very old and our members are protected by the Guardians and Fierce Devis of the Sampradaya or line of initiation. If in a difficult pass as a result of your experiments you may call on the Line to protect you.

Psychokinesis

A way of moving objects by the power of the mind or by psychic means. Much in the news in the last decade because of the tricks of Uri Geller and other forkbenders. Remember that skilled conjurors are capable of producing effects which seem to baffle the mind and defy explanation. If such things were possible there would be no need for governments to spend millions of pounds on weapon technology. This point also applies to other psychic 'abilities'.

It is known that both the US and the USSR governments have sponsored research into psychic abilities - but such experiments are only

The Apprentice

to be expected and do not necessarily mean that government agencies believe they work. All avenues are investigated.

Auras

Many ancient traditions aver that individuals have a field of psychic energy capable of being discerned by sensitive individuals. However this subject too suffers from too much literature and not enough practical experimentation.

Beware of literature which gives 'pat' meanings to aura colours. Every individual differs. This subject is different from 'charisma' which every Amookos member should cultivate.

Bioenergy

Bioenergy, life-energy, Chi or whatever term given refers to the subtle energy which seems to mark the difference between a corpse and a living human being. This energy seems to be of a fuidic nature and can be blocked in its passage by muscular or mental blocks. The AMOOKOS aim is to have it flowing freely and available at all times. The Tantrik term for it is *Prana-Shakti*, the energy or shakti which is related intimately to the processing of food, breath and impressions. When She leaves one's body one normally dies.

Further Reading

Ecstasy, Equipoise and Eternity by H H Shri Gurudeva Mahendrahanatha. This MS is, in effect the history lecture of AMOOKOS.

Twilight Yoga This publication, indispensible for AMOOKOS members, now includes the important paper the *Navanaths*, plus additional material.

Footnotes

(1) The armour includes the whole region of the neck and shoulders, the three eyes being the two physical eyes plus the 'third eye' in the forehead.
(2) See "On Shambhala", page 28
(3) Vajra means a lightning bolt
(4) The dictum 'as above so below' is central to our work in Amookos. This is discussed in depth in the third degree.

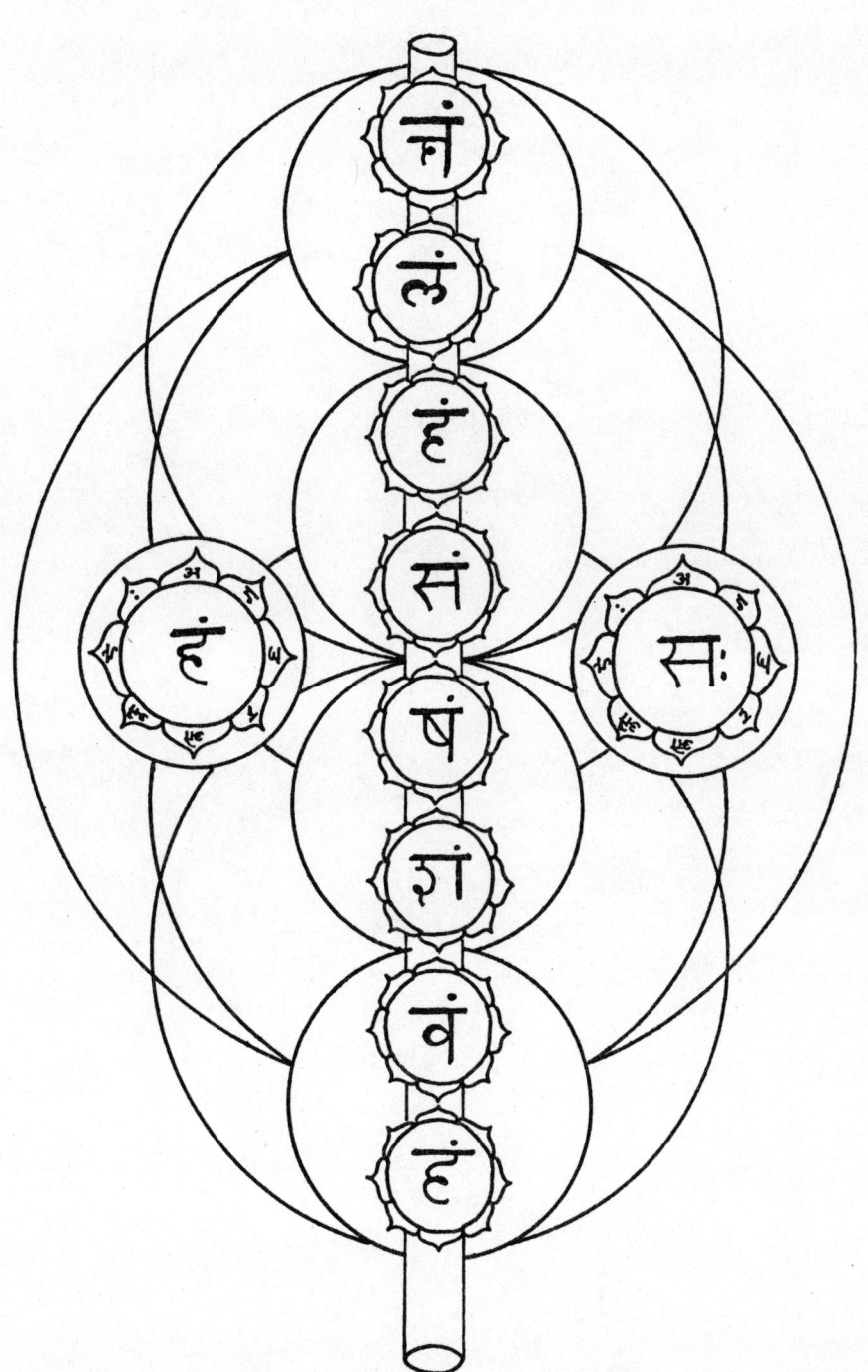

Chapter Two: Esquires and Handmaidens

Symbolism of the Grade

Staff:
This is an instrument of support identical to the Lingam or Meru-Lingam which supports the Cosmos. In the body of a magician it is the central core or pivot about which is woven the web of Maya (or illusion)-producing Shaktis of the physical and psychic complex.

Gem:
Opal, the colour of semen, the marrow of the staff

Lingam:
Wooden

Study:
Sustained practice and meditation of the 2nd degree material

Necklace:
Wooden

Number of beads:
6

Zonule name:
Circle

Animal:
A black dog. The black dog is the vehicle of Bhairava, the terrific aspect of Adinath-shiva. An Iconograph showing Dattatreya shows Him to be surrounded by four dogs.

Place of meeting:
Rooms

Tantra Magick

To each Esquire and Handmaiden the Magician makes the following known:

The treasures of the world are lures to the foolish, but those who aim for the light seek to own but little of this mundane world.

If you are born to be a Master you will discover this scroll in the archives of heaven; but as a churl to live you will never find it.

Since nothing is enjoyed in Necropolis, it is better to die young and attained than grow old in sleep and die as an ignorant fool.

Instead of a life of sleep, awake to life! Instead of dreams, nightmares, drudgery and boredom, awake to the fullness of the real Cosmic life!

An expanding view of a fantastic Cosmos must have its counterpart in a fantastic view of New Life, Living, Lust and Awakened Love.

If you want power over mankind - teach them to sleep, to trust and have faith; never to think or awaken from the toil which is their joy.

When you ask questions you reveal your ignorance. Yet this is good, for those who ask no questions will remain ignorant forever.

Esquires and Handmaidens

Working the Grade

Time Lore

Reread the section on AMOOKOS astrology in the first degree. A copy of *Tantrik Astrology*[1] should be obtained.

It is essential that you grasp the major differences between Tropical Zodiac (TZ) and Sidereal Zodiac (SZ).

AMOOKOS Time Lore is founded on the following alchemical principles:

- that which is above is like that which is below (Macro Micrcosmos);
- every natural process in the Cosmos is based on the same natural laws as every other process - learn from nature;
- one's own true Being or Spirit or Shiva particle is free from time. We can see Time as Shakti.

All planets, constellations, and planetary aspects in an Amookos breath chart (or horoscope) can become the powers and energies of an Adinath. Usually they enslave a person by unconscious identification, caused by the breath taking on a certain rhythm at birth. One may be their Master or Mistress (Nath).

In the rosary of a Nath there are 108 beads. In an Amookos breath chart there are 108 parts of the Moon.

The Body Yantra

Introduction

You must make very serious efforts to understand this symbol, as on it much of the AMOOKOS curriculum depends.

In essence the Body Yantra is a simplified Shri Yantra. The dot in the centre or bindu represents Adinatha, that is to say Consciousness-Awareness.

The triangle in the centre has as its angles Shiva ☉ Shakti ☾ and Shiva-Shakti ☽. The points of the triangle are also the three *gunas* or qualities of Indian Philosophy - Rajas, Tamas and Sattvas.

We can summarize and expand this information in the following table:

ACTIVE	PASSIVE	RECONCILING	
Rajas	*Tamas*	*Sattvas*	(3 gunas)
Sun	Moon	Earth	
Father	Mother	Child	

Tantra Magick

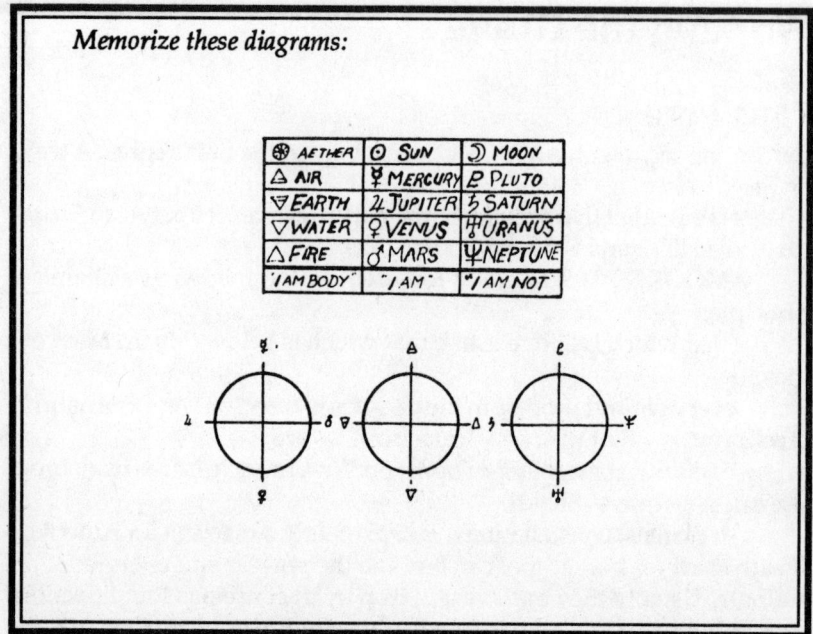

Memorize these diagrams:

Strive to expand this table by yourself. It has to be stressed that these three fundamental qualities cannot be studied in isolation, nor do they exist except in relationship with each other. The whole triangle can also be seen as the circle of Adinatha's Shaktis or Energies called Will (*Iccha*), Knowledge (*Jnana*) Action (*Kriya*).

We have to examine these powers in a practical way. Will is also determination, resolution. Knowledge is know-how, lack of ignorance about any given thing. Action is the means of accomplishing what is willed.

To take a practical example: to bake a cake you have to set the objective and be prepared to carry it through to the end, despite any obstacles. This is Will.

You have to know how to do it - the recipe, oven setting, etc.

You have to actually do it! You have to use instruments, the bowl, the oven, the mixing spoon. You have to assemble the required materials.

Only in this way through the combination of the three, can the desired object be brought into existence. Therefore, before undertaking any project you are asked as an AMOOKOS member to firstly make a powerful resolution to carry things through. Secondly you must ensure that you have the necessary knowledge. Thirdly you must do it. You should apply these three Shaktis in every endeavour. Apply this to all

Esquires and Handmaidens

and everything.

You will see from this that the most basic yantra from which all others proceed is •

It symbolises the union of the three Shaktis.

The Body Yantra shown on page 44, consists of five circles or mandalas:
1 The Bindu, potential, Adinath
2 The Triangle
3 Circle of eight petals (planets)
4 Circle of twelve petals (constellations)
5 Square of four gates or the magickal enclosure

It is the central triangle which gives rise to the various modifications shown by the petals. In this second degree we will be working with a yantra in which the circle of twelve petals is omitted.

A yantra can be constructed in two ways:

Bhu (Skt, Earth) Flat, 2-dimensional

Meru (Skt, a Mountain) Rising to a point or pyramid

The Body Yantra illustrated above has twenty-seven points of Energy; from the outside working in they are four elements, twelve Constellations, eight planets, three fundamental qualities, (as described above). The bindu, which is identical with you, the wizard upon the dragon Seat, is outside Time or Space, and has no number or characteristics except Consciousness-Awareness. It is the True Being, or Spirit, or Shiva Particle.

These twenty-seven points of energy are also the letters of the alphabet, counting the blank space as an additional character. They are the root of all mantra.

The number twenty-seven is of some importance to AMOOKOS work, and its value and significance will become steadily apparent to you. It is a key which unlocks and unblocks human psychology - as it does so it draws together all the elements of our Tradition.

The circle of the eight planets shows a modification of the points Shiva and Shakti. The table below shows how these emanate from each other

A	B	C	D	E	F	G	H	I
J	K	L	M	N	O	P	Q	R
S	T	U	V	W	X	Y	Z	&
1	2	3	4	5	6	7	8	9
☿	♆	♂	☽	☉	♃	♀	♄	♅

Tantra Magick

The Body Yantra should be thought of as a mapping of Macrocosm onto the Microcosm, here for example, the cosmos onto the body: this is summarized in the legendary Emerald Tablet of Hermes Trismegistos:

"I speak not fictitious things, but that which is certain and most true. What is below is like that which is above. What is above is like that which is below. This accomplishes the miracle of the One Thing."

As initiates of a spiritual tradition you may centre yourselves on the Dragon Seat or Bindu and recreate your Cosmos.

In the natural course of human development the Cosmos is in Chaos. This is where we must connect with the Freemasons, whose motto is 'Order out of Chaos'. Through AMOOKOS we guide the sincere to achieve this for themselves.

Sun-Moon-Fire Meditation

In the first degree Grade Papers is an illustration of the Chalice of Shambhala, or Shambhala Vajra. You were asked to meditate on these three great Lights of sun, moon and fire (page 23).

The realization of these Three in One is one of our great secrets.

Moon is Knowledge and Intellect

Sun is emotional Feeling and Will

Fire is bodily Sensation and Action

The question you have to ask yourself is: What is the fourth?

A Nath is a human of higher intellect who gives equal importance to these three in Her or His being. For such a person the world may be held in the palm of the hand. It should be clearly understood that education emphasizes only one of these lights - knowledge.

This disaster produces psychopaths and sociopaths devoid of feeling and bodily sensation. The Chalice of Shambhala, or Shambhala Vajra, into which is poured the Nectar of Adinatha is one unified Whole. Part of your task in this grade is to correct the imbalance in your own nature, to uncover the Moon.

Meditate for ten minutes daily on the following points: do I feel my body? Do I sense my emotions? Use everyday experience to help you. Try and feel every part of your body.

Ayurveda and the Three Qualities

There is a Nath Yoga Tantrik system of 'medicine' little known in the West. It is called *Ayurveda*. For a human to be healthy her or his body, made of the three Qualities, should be in harmony. For this to occur a body requires food. There are three kinds of food:

Esquires and Handmaidens

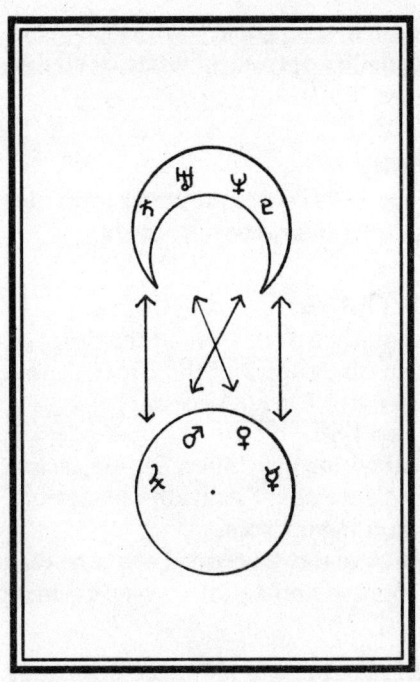

Moon   Sense Impressions
Sun   Breath
Fire   Food and Water

They can only be enjoyed if there is an enjoyer present to enjoy them.

The instruments by which the enjoyer consumes that to be enjoyed are known as the three Fires:

Moon   Fire of Sense Metabolism - the five senses

Sun   Fire of Breath Metabolism - lung and blood interchange

Fire   Fire of Food Metabolism - stomach, etc

An important difference

This is a table of Growth and Decay, or Creation-Maintenance-Destruction. From it we can learn self-understanding, and you will find the table is a map of the development of a child from conception to the age of about 5 or 6. As we stressed above, each natural process can tell us a great deal about every other natural process. Here the correspondence is shown between a child and the planetary system.

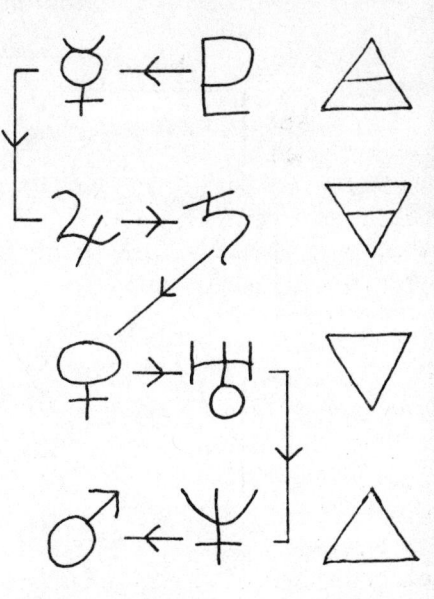

Tantra Magick

between a Nath and an ordinary person in the ordinary world is that the former may enjoy whilst the latter usually does not. Meditate on all this with an open heart.

Unity of Knowledge and Being

Strive to understand that the Grade Papers of the Order form one complete whole, and attempt to discover their interrelationship.

Magickal Ritual of the Body Yantra

The main rite of the Body Yantra should be performed at the times of Full, New and Quarters of the moon. In Magick of the Great Yantra consideration of the Tortoise Body (page 18) is not necessary.

Open as in the first degree (steps 1-5).

Being seated on the Dragon Seat within the Umbra Zonule, facing East, visualize yourself as being of the nature of Adinath-Shiva, pure consciousness, the Fourth, the eternal Lingam Yoni.

Draw in front of you the yantra as in the diagram. It could be that you have already had this design engraved on a pure metal, in which

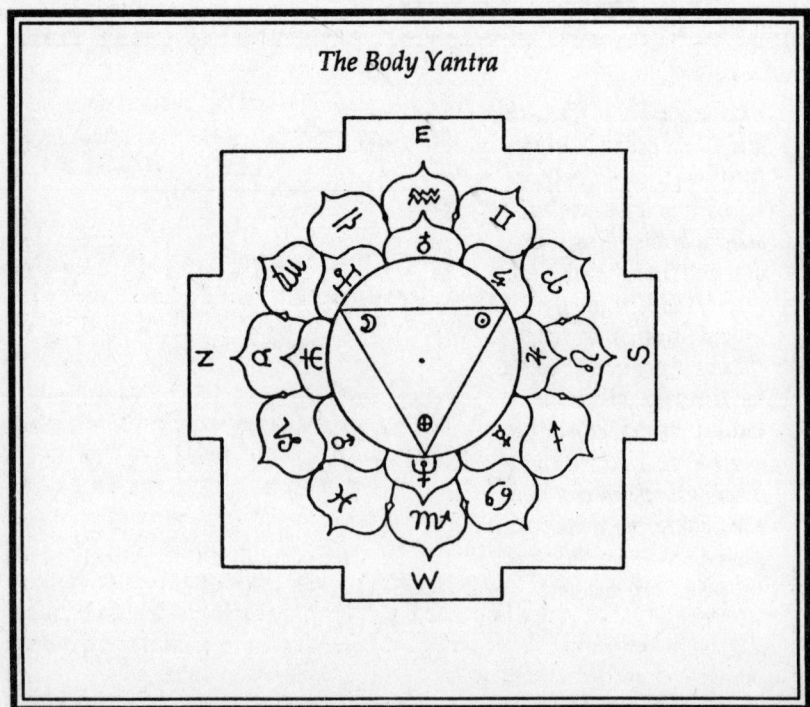

The Body Yantra

Esquires and Handmaidens

case this may be used.

Take a red flower, or red powder (Kum Kum) and visualize that the essence of Shakti is carried via your breath, and breathe it onto the flower or powder. Take the flower or powder to the centre of the yantra and say the mantra:

Om Hrim Shrim Krim Parameshvari Svaha

Consider that Adinath and Shakti are now in reality placed on the Bindu or Potential, central Point of the Yantra. Offer food, water and any other pleasant things to Adinath and Shakti, saying:

I offer.....to White Adinath and his Red Shakti of Time in the Bindu of the Yantra.

The following Ritual Practice may be accomplished in two ways, either from the centre to the outside (Projection), or the outside to the centre (Absorption). When doing a Rite of Projection start with Kriya Shakti in the centre of the Yantra. If performing a Rite of Absorption, start from the outside, taking Asita Shakti the Goddess of Midnight first.

Offer food, water and other pleasant substances to each of the attendants of Shiva Shakti (respectively) saying:

Om Hrim Shrim Krim I offer....to (Name of attendant).

Visualise the Shaktis as follows. Each Shakti should be visualized as embracing their respective Shiva. Each of the Shivas are white, naked, smeared with ashes, with erect penises. The attribution of these Shaktis to the Body Yantra is shown in the diagram.

Kriya Shakti (Spirit): She is black as fertile earth, clothed in space, with 3 eyes and 2 hands, garlanded in sapphires and smeared with purple unguent, with a smiling face and dark eyes, the embodiment of Action.

Jnana Shakti (Moon): Of the whiteness of Snow, with a beautiful and pleasant face, three eyes, giving boons and dispelling fear with Her two hands, wearing a necklace and ornaments of white pearls. She is the embodiment of Knowledge.

Iccha Shakti (Sun): Red as a million suns, three eyes, two hands. She wears rudraksha berries and rubies, is smeared with red powder, youthful, with high swelling breasts, wearing golden bracelets and anklets. She is the embodiment of Will.

Pita Devi (Mercury): Slim, with restless eyes, naked, smeared with yellow powder, wearing a quartz necklace, holding in Her right hand a book and in Her left hand a mirror, the embodiment of Thought.

Nila Shakti (Pluto): Naked, violet in colour, that bizarre one, almost invisible because of Her darkness, wearing gems of black jet, holding in Her right hand a bowl full of shattered glass and in Her left hand a mask, the embodiment of detachment.

Tantra Magick

Rakta Devi (Mars): Worship that red and slender Amazon with narrow hips and small breasts, naked, of angry face, three eyes, holding in Her right hand a sharp knife and in Her left hand a small shield, the embodiment of Vigour.

Aruna Shakti (Neptune): Naked, with three gazelle-like eyes, and long dark hair, that being of dreams who wears gems of opal and holds in Her right hand a bowl which smokes, and in Her left hand a skrying crystal, the embodiment of imagination.

Harina Devi (Venus): A most beautiful Goddess with three eyes and two hands, a sweetly smiling face, large lovely breasts, slender of waist, most beautifully rounded in form, with fair hair, holding in Her right hand a flower and with Her left hand making the sign of giving, the embodiment of Love.

Karbura Devi (Uranus): Worship that Large Lady with three eyes, angular and haughty, wearing a necklace of crystal, smeared with blue dust, holding threateningly in Her right hand a stick, and with Her left hand holding a child to one of Her breasts, the embodiment of Control.

Malini Devi (Jupiter): Worship the sweet Lady who is naked, wearing the best kind of gold and jewels, with a smiling face, Her tongue out and touching Her lower lip, with three eyes. With Her right hand

Esquires and Handmaidens

She showers gold onto Her worshipper; in Her left hand She holds a bowl full of choice food, the embodiment of Expansion.

Asita Shakti (Saturn): Worship the old, dark and resentful Lady, with dishevelled hair and melancholy of aspect. She has three eyes and two hands, naked with Her rough body and pendulous breasts, smeared with black dust. She holds in Her right hand a cord with which She restrains, and in Her left hand She holds a skull, the great Devi who is the embodiment of Restriction.

The Devis of the Elements

The forms of the Great Devis of the Elements are like those in the Opening Rite. Each is seated on Her Shiva-Beast. Ritual accessories should be offered to each of these great Eternities in turn. When these Devis, with their Shivas, have thus been worshipped, once again one should offer good things to Shiva and Shakti in the centre of the yantra.

Now recite the mantra *Om Hrim Shrim Krim Parameshvari Svaha* six times (or as many times as the beads on your Grade Rosary). Meditate for a while, and take the flower or some of the powder back to your face, and imagine that the Essence is once again taken back into your being to become one with you.

Close as on page 20 of first degree.

Preparing a Permanent Body Yantra

If you wish to prepare a permanent Body Yantra, the following notes may be of use.

A gold yantra lasts for life, a silver yantra for twelve years, and one painted on cloth or good paper for six years. If painted, the colours used should be those of the Goddesses (see diagram). Alternatively a new Yantra may be traced each time.

Consecration of a Permanent Yantra.

The Timing of the Ritual: You should choose the exact moment of an eclipse, or a Sun conjunct with Moon, but ensure that there are no malefics in the Angles of the chart or aspecting the Sun or Moon, consider only Conjunction, Opposition or Square in these assessments.

You will also need to consecrate water.[2] Open your Umbra Zonule in the usual way. Face East. Place your Yantra flat on a pedestal of red silk or cotton. Meditate for a while on yourself as one with the Sun and the Moon, the embodiment of Consciousness. Draw your breath via red or white powder onto the Yantra.[3]

Say:

Tantra Magick

Om I bow to Shiva Shakti.
Om Hamsa, may this Yantra be alive!
Om Hamsa may this Yantra breathe!
Om Hamsa may this Yantra have all the senses!
Om Hamsa may this Yantra have speech, mind eyes, ears, tongue, nose!
Om Hamsa may happiness dwell here forever!

Then pour over the Yantra our Kaula Nectar (consecrated water) and heaps of white ash. Take its essence afterwards back into your heart via breath.

Clean the Yantra carefully and wrap it in silk or cotton (preferably red).

Subsidiary Practices of the Body Yantra

Each of the eight planetary Shaktis has a Yantra similar in form to the main Yantra. Thus eight by eight are the sixty-four shaktis. So Moon, Sun and fire (Iccha, Jnana and Kriya) are in the central triangle of the yantras of each of the following, and the four Protectresses of the Fortress are in the four corners.

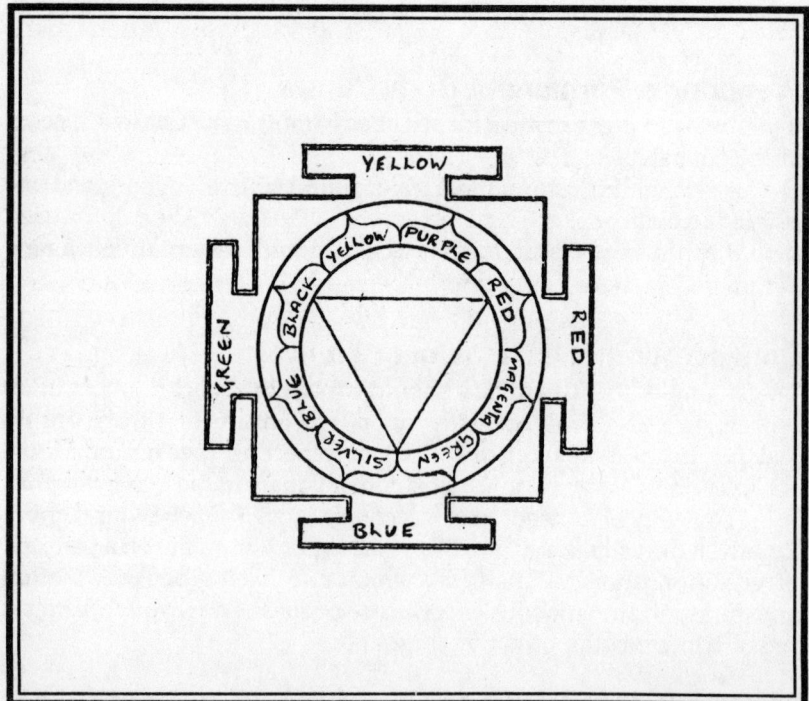

Esquires and Handmaidens

Pitadevi: The Yellow Goddess
She rules ambiguity, herbs, cleverness, language, alliance, speed, duality. Her secret name is 'look forward, never back'. When She is invoked into Her Yantra her eight yoginis, all similar to her, are Skill, Acuteness, Duplicity, Leopardess, Authoress, Craftswoman, Brightness, Impulse. The Yantra should be coloured yellow.

Nila shakti: The Sapphire Shakti
Masks, shock, detachment, isolation, hermits, anchorites are ruled by Her. Her secret name is "I do not exist". Her attendants are Isolation, Hermit, Detachment, Darkness, Mask, Vampire, Death, Split.

Raktadevi: The Red Goddess
She rules all things signified by the names of her attendants. They are Anger, Stamina, Blood, Knife, Castrator, Murderer, Conqueror, Vigorous. Colour Her Yantra blood-red, and approach Her with devoted mind.

Arunashakti: The Magenta Shakti
The attendants' names signify the Powers (Shaktis) of the Goddess. They are Romantic One, Dreamer, Passive, Confused One, Undecided, Misty, Serpent Girl, Roe Deer. Her Yantra is magenta coloured.

Harinadevi: The Green Goddess
She is the sweet Goddess of Love and Affection. In the petals of Her Green Yantra are Synthesis, Harmony, Placidity, Joyfulness, Love's Ointment, Adorned with Peacock Feathers, Whore, Artist

Karburadevi: The Grey Goddess
Her attendants who resemble Her, are Analysis, Control, Love's Screw, Dominatrix, Count, Hierarchy, Compulsive One, Robot. She gives control over all things, and her Yantra should be coloured silver.

Malinidevi: Flower Goddess
She, the great Giver of Wealth, gives wealth on every level. Her attendants are Tongue, Assimilator, Expansion, Optimistic One, Vain, Fortune, Largesse, Generosity. Each should be worshipped in order. The Yantra is blue.

Asitadevi: The Black Goddess
Offer obeisance to the Great Limiter with her eight attendants known as Rejection, Limitation, Caution, Responsibility, Melancholy, Servitude, Sorrow, Darkness. The Dusky One, with Her magickal cord, restrains and punishes all. Her Yantra is black.

Tantra Magick

The Magickal Powers of the Eight Planetary Devis, and the timing of their rituals

Pita Devi. Works of knowledge, Mercury should be conjunct Ascendant or Midheaven, square[4] with Moon. There must be no malefics (see *Tantrik Astrology* for more details). Mercury in Gemini or Virgo Rashi or Navamsha.

Nila Shakti. Works of detachment. Pluto must be conjunct the Midheaven. No malefics.

Rakta Devi. Works of destruction. Mars must be in Aries or Capricorn and angular, conjunct or opposing the moon.

Aruna Shakti. Works of Dream, Hypnosis and Deluding. Neptune angular on its own.

Harina Devi. Works of Love and Sexuality. Venus in Pisces, Libra conjunct Asc or Angle square Moon. No malefics.

Karbura Devi. Works of control. Uranus in angle, no malefics.

Malini Devi. Works of Wealth. Jupiter in Pisces, Sagittarius or Cancer or on angle, no malefics. Square Moon as well if this is possible.

Asita Devi. Works of Death. Saturn angular.

Ritual Work

Before worshiping any of these attendants of the Great Shakti of Time you must first perform the Great Ritual of the Body Yantra. Then draw a Yantra appropriate to the particular Shakti, and Her worship is accomplished in a similar way, substituting Her subsidiary attendants for the eight planetary Shaktis.

Work in these lesser Yantras should be performed on similar lines as the Great Body Yantra. The magician has to win their love to gain success. This implies repeated practice and also suitable offerings. In the case of the Yellow Goddess, yellow flowers, yellow powder, yellow cloth, etc are to be used.

The Body Yantra and the Tradition of Tantra

The Body Yantra is a *Kalachakra Yantra* - one that deals with the Wheel of Time, and is a synthesis of the Yantras of the Devis or Goddesses Kali and Lalita.

The eight yoginis on the eight petals of the Yantra represent the eight planets Pluto, Mercury, Jupiter Saturn, Venus, Uranus, Neptune, Mars. Three Yoginis in the central triangle represent Moon Sun and Fire. Four yoginis on the gates of the diagram represent the four elements, or the four twilights. The bindu or point in the centre of the Body Yantra is Shiva-Shakti-Samarasa (Sexual Union) or Perfect Assimilation. It is

Esquires and Handmaidens

from their union that the whole Yantra proceeds.

When actually performing the ritual, you should spend a considerable period visualizing the Goddess as residing in one's heart, The visualize her being 'drawn out' of your body by your breath and placed in the centre of the Yantra. Once She has been invoked into the centre, the rest of the ritual must proceed as if She were actually present in the Yantra. So one should bow to Her, give Her flowers, fruit, and other suitable things, and finally give Her your own complex of Yoginis.

As the Devi resides in your body surrounded by her Yoginis (which people mistakenly take to be their own powers), the ritual is an affirmation of a situation which can actually be taken to exist at all times. Adinath Shiva, free from Time, the Witness, has no powers or energies. It is Devi only who enjoys, feels, thinks, etc, etc.

In this particular ritual you are taking the Devi as in one of her Particular aspects as Lady of Time. The affirmation or offering could therefore take the form:

O Devi, I give you my body (Earth), emotions (Sun), mind (Moon), vigour (Mars), imagination (Neptune), sense of analysis (Uranus), affection (Venus), sorrow (Saturn) happiness (Jupiter), sense of logic (Mercury), sense of detachment (Pluto). Take my whole day (Dawn, Midday, Sunset, Midnight) and my whole night.

Offerings to the Devi

In this ritual anything may be offered to the Devi when She is seated in the centre of the Yantra. Every tantric tradition insists that animal sacrifice should be given to the Devi. The mantra *Svaha* at the end of a string of Bija[5] mantras indicates this sacrifice. If an animal is offered, it is said that it must be male. This is because the sadhaka or magician is taken as male. The highest sacrifice is a human being, and only kings may perform this sacrifice.

Traditionally, Tantra tells us that the 'King' is a Vira or Hero who is prepared to offer his life to Devi. 'Man' represents pride or ego. We can see other animals represent other egotistic qualities like greed, for instance, a tortoise is lethargy, a bull is stubbornness, etc.

In a Kalachakra rite the little animals of the zodiac together with their Kleshas [6] may be offered as sacrifice.

Ram represents hastiness; Bull is stubbornness; Twins are scatteredness or lack of concentration; Cancer is isolation; Leo is fury; Virgo is fussiness; Libra is sloppiness; Scorpio is secretiveness; Sagittarius is orthodoxy; Capricorn is making difficulties for self or other; Aquarius is gloominess; Pisces is delusion.

Tantra Magick

If you don't give animal sacrifice on the lines mentioned above, it is said that Devi takes you instead.

It is only fools who think that blood of innocent creatures has to be shed during this rite. The blood you shed is your own.

Structure of the ritual

We may divide the Ritual of the Body Yantra into three main parts:

1   the inner visualization, preceded by the 'cleaning of the working area'
2   the invocation, accompanied with offering of everything that is red - "menstrual flowers", "blood of animals", "red flowers", etc.
3   The closing rite, taking the Goddess back into your own being and 'tidying up the leftovers'

These components are common to every Indian Tantrik tradition. Although Tantra is associated in the West with Devi or the Goddess, there are Tantras of Shiva, Vishnu, Ganapati, Surya, Kartikeya and many other aspects of the Primordial God and Goddess. All of them employ the same structure for ritual there are variations - for example while we invoke the great Shakti of Time into her Yantra, Shiva is invoked into a stone representing the penis, Vishnu into a spiral stone (Shalagrama) Ganapati into a red stone, etc, etc. But whatever the base, the ritual dynamic remains the same.

It is important not to be misled about ritual. In the West, which is relatively ritual-free, esotericists tend to think that simply doing a ritual accomplishes what is desired. This might even be justified by calling the ritual a 'spell'. But a ritual is iconographic. Its form and structure tell us many things about the people who devised it. For this reason rituals should not be altered indiscriminately.

So deep thought and pondering about the structure and components of a ritual is a necessity for a Tantrik. After all, many millions of ordinary folk in India perform Tantrik rituals without any understanding of their dynamics. This means that people are pacing out magick circles, performing banishing rituals, using Yantras.

So you should very carefully examine the structure of the Body Yantra Ritual with all its elements for an understanding of its purpose and aims. To simply take them on face value is to miss their point. [7]

Amulet of the Great Goddess of Time

You may read this amulet or armour during the rite as an offering to the Goddess installed in the Yantra. It may, alternatively be written on paper, and the Goddess installed into it, later to be worn on the person.

Esquires and Handmaidens

Alternatively it may be used as a rite of general protection when recited at one of the four twilights.

Om
May Shiva with his shakti of Time protect me in my heart!
May the Shakti of Knowledge protect my brain!
May the Shakti of Action protect my genitals!
Nila Shakti protect my brain, Pita Devi shield my forehead!
Malini-Devi, dance on my tongue! Asita Devi, protect my throat!
May Harina Devi and Karbura Devi protect and shield my anus!
May Arunashakti and Raktadevi protect my genitals!
May the sixty-four Yoginis shield and guard my limbs always and everywhere!
Dawn shield me in the East!
Sunset shield me in the West!
Midday protect me in the South!
Midnight protect me in the North!
May the Shakti of Will protect me above and below!
Om Hrim Shrim Krim Parameshvari Svaha!

Work with Mnemonics and Their Significance

This is a Gateway to the Laboratory: inside is a subscience: Association of Thought

If you have sincerely worked with the material in the first degree papers you have made a start. Hopefully you have already perfected the minimal technique.

Most or many of people's memory content is associated randomly. Every person is different. For one person 'cabbage' may be associated with the pleasures of the country. For another it might evoke the memory of school dinners.

Much of that which passes for 'wide awake' consists of a string of apparently random associations.

We start off thinking one thing, and before we know what has happened our thought has diverged and gone in any number of directions.

There is no point attempting to stop the flow of thoughts. You must simply observe them very minutely. Do this on a daily basis. Be sure to record the details in your diary of magick. A clue to this is that something observed, heard, touched, smelled, tasted can trigger off a whole chain of internal associations which 'bring back the past', and thus bridge memory.

Tantra Magick

Remember: The word is not the thing, but just a label for it. The map is not the territory!

The following exercise is given in order that insight may be obtained into thought association. It is quite possible by this method to memorize a list of 100 words or things easily, within a period of no more than 15 minutes to half an hour.

Instead of rhyming numbers 1-10 as before, we turn the numbers from 11 to 100 or further, into words by assigning to each digit a consonant.

1=t, 2=n, 3=m, 4=r, 5=l, 6=d, 7=c,k, 8=f,v, 9=p,b, 0=s,z.

By doing this we can insert vowels to make words linked to numbers, eg, 11 = tEAt, 12 = tIn, 13=tOmE, 14=tAr, etc, etc. It is now easy to use these triggers in the same way as before.

This method may also be used to memorize long series of numbers.

123273024641 = tIn mAn cOmEs in rEd rat

When you have prepared your list of triggers up to 100 find some way of using them positively. You could memorize the meanings of the 78 tarot cards, the 64 I Ching hexagrams, whatever you wish.

You should now be in a position to expand this system for other uses in the field of memory and it will also prove worthwhile to spend some time in considering what significance it has in the realm of association of thought.

The Five Kleshas

Read this Thrice:
> *The Five Pain bearing Obstructions*
> *The Root Causes of Trouble and Strife*
> *Ignorance-Ego-Revulsion-Attachment-Clinging to Life*

"By means of the fivefold bonds called Kleshas, Shankara binds the pashus. On being served well by devotion, He alone is their redeemer. The five Kleshas that have become fetters are Ignorance, Ego, Attraction, Revulsion, Clinging to Life".

(Linga Purana, II, 9)

Practical work with these five obstacle blocks is a major secret of the Nath tradition. This part of your work stems from a very ancient and central tradition within the Sampradaya (or line of initiation). The 5 Ob Blocks must be combatted individually, and their tangled ramifications

Esquires and Handmaidens

within us should be the subject of repeated meditation and study.

This work is very inner. If you do not yet have a copy of *Twilight Yoga* you should obtain one.

1. Ignorance

This can take many forms. For example, thinking we know what is real when we have no basis for such a thought. Remember the five sensory joys of a Knight Of Shambhala: the five senses refined and awakened. As a conditioned product it is certain that you suffer to a greater of lesser extent from the drug called hypnosis. Your senses are dull and base, and you sense only what you are conditioned to sense. This is only one aspect of the Ignorance Ob-Block. If your senses are obscured, how can it be possible to perceive what is real or imaginary.

2. Ego

The imaginary opinion we have of ourselves which can also take many varied forms. The idea that we are capable or incapable of some or many things which the evidence of our actions contradict. This opinion may be deflated (masochism) or inflated (narcissism). Either way it is not true. Ask yourself what has given birth to such a monster? Do your words, appearance, or whatever you 'value' about yourself compensate for a stultified inner existence? Are you such a wondrous being that none of this could possibly apply to you? Investigate, experiment and verify.

3. Revulsion

Nothing in itself is horrible, but our attitude of mind gives it its colour. How many things do you dislike simply because you are conditioned? Customs, local mores and ethics are all rejected by the Kaula Nath. If you are repulsed by anything trace it back to its root. How did you know it was horrible? Who told you? The natural person acting spontaneously has no need of conditioned ideas. One of Shiva's names is "Aghora" meaning nothing in itself is horrible. Conditioned by the revulsion Klesha we set ourselves artificial limits.

4. Attachment

The false idea that we possess anything. "This is mine." Identification with all sorts of ideas, things, people. The inability to realize that we are as much a part of nature as the things we claim for our own. The inability to realize that it is what we need - rather than what we want - which is important.

5. Clinging to Life

Refusing to submit to natural laws. Trying to make two go into three or refusal to accept the inevitable. Lack of ability to surrender, or to give in. This has many undesirable side-effects, including the inability to give ourselves to anything or anyone.

Working on these Ob-Blocks is an essential element of the Wisdom Teaching of Amookos. Now is the time to start dissolving the five kleshas with their entanglements.

You cannot be a master until you have tackled the Ob-Blocks in yourself, and there can be no magick with them. The Kleshas apply on many levels and are in fact the horrible shadows of the pure elements. We will discuss this further in chapter three. Reach to their essence and you are free of them.

The Human Multichord

We may see the human frame as containing a multitude of stringed instruments, each of which vibrates at a certain rate. Many will be found by the wise to be out of tune. In some cases this disharmony can wreck the whole.

Unnecessarily tense muscles can rob a person of energy. In most cases the muscle groups which are chronically tense will be unconscious - that is, we are unaware of them.

These tensions, judged as a collective or aggregate, form armours, nets or types which may permit no free expression and preclude the inflow and outflow of mother nature in her many forms.

Nets or armours fall into distinct groups in accordance with Time-Breath Science. See the section on Time Lore in the first Grade paper: popularly this is known as an individual's horoscope. This matter is discussed in some detail later and in the book *Tantrik Astrology* (see bibliography). An individual approach based on accurate knowledge is essential.

The armours fall into two categories depending on their relation to Sun and Moon; Hard and Soft. The three Shaktis of Sun, Moon and Fire in a person form a triple octave so that which is structured in bodily tension is also reflected intellectually and in the emotions.

For these reasons a purely intellectual or one-sided approach to problems, pathologies and conditioning fails. Tendencies to armouring are birth born.

We must never forget that we are, in Tantrik terminology, Heroines and Heroes. The inner and oral tradition is that Yoginis and Shaktis exist simply for the purpose of keeping our minds off these problems. So resolution is of the utmost importance, as we are on the path of return. Why is it said that the Kaula Nath way is as narrow as a razor edge? It is because we are willfully setting ourselves as Heroines and Heroes in a battle we must win, but which the ordinary person cannot even face.

Esquires and Handmaidens

Academy of symbolism

The Significance of Dattatreya
(Initiates of AMOOKOS were given a copy of the Dattatreya Upanishad, translated into English, and published in the Adyar Library Series.[8])

Upanishad means secret or esoteric doctrine - oral lore. There are said to be one hundred and eight Upanishads, this being an ideal number. The Dattatreya Upanishad is assimilated to the fourth or so called Magickal Veda - Atharva Veda.

Veda means knowledge or ritual lore. An Upanishad may have nothing to do with religion. It is either genuine magickal lore, or, in some cases an attempt to imitate the genuine article. Many Upanishads present a whole body of the highest or spiritual esoteric lore in the briefest space.

Dattatreya is credited with being an enlightened being who was the first expounder of the Agamas and Tantras. He is the alleged author of the Avadhoot Gita and it the promulgator of the Shri Vidya. He is the Guru or Guide figure of all India, the prototype of all Yogis and Sadhus, and the legendary founder of the Naths.

He is mentioned in sacred texts, such as Upanishads, Puranas and Tantras. In the *Shrimad Bhagavata* a large section deals with him as Avadhoot [9]. Modern images of Dattatreya often show him clothed. This panders to a modern puritanism and modesty, for of old and by tradition he is always spoken of as completely naked.

A whole lore exists on this nakedness. The Sanskrit word is *digambara*, meaning clothed with the directions of Space.

Many legends are associated with him, although very few have so far been translated into English. Very often he is said to appear to people as naked, chewing betel, with a naked Shakti on his left lap, eating hog meat and drinking wine.

We can learn from this that he is a figure having little to do with orthodoxy. The pig is abhorred in India. Wine is said by the orthodox to be under Brahma's curse. Nakedness is prohibited by the Right Hand or Orthodox. Datta is the eternal Shaman, Shiva himself, rejecting all useless rules and living according to his own True Will or Law. This is Svecchacharya - the Path of Own Will.

At least one thousand years before Buddha, Lord Datta is said to have achieved enlightenment under the Audumber Tree. It is possible that this early legend gave rise to the Buddhist story.

The image of Dattatreya can tell us something about his significance and occult meaning. He has three heads, six arms, stands on the world, is flanked by a cow, and surrounded by four dogs. He wears red padukas (wooden sandals). His six arms hold trident, discus, conch, lotus, mace, water-pot.

The Inner significance of these symbols

The three Gunas, or qualities - the three heads. Brahma - Holy Creation. Vishnu - Holy Maintenance. Shiva - Holy Withdrawal.

Trident - three eyes and three gunas. Conch - spiral levogyrate. Discus - cosmos. Mace - sovereignty. Lotus - blossoming expansion of the Cosmos. Waterpot - Sadhu's vessel.

Cow - Shakti. The World Cosmos. The four dogs - the four directions of Bhairava or Shiva. The whole image represents an individual or human being who combines all things, all conditions, all words, all states - in other words a realized One. He is free from all worldly conditions - hence he is naked, moving in the world or remaining still according to his Own Will. Therefore he is the supreme Magician. The Cosmic Shaman.

Today Datta is often worshipped or propitiated as a god. This process often happens to people in India. Datta is especially popular in the regions Saurashtra and Maharashtra. In the South of India he is the focus of a purely devotional cult.

The Academy of the Five Senses

You must take the practices described here very seriously and make conscientious efforts to adhere to the six month schedule.

The word "Academy" is derived from Akademos, a Greek demigod who gave his name to the garden in which Plato taught his followers. Now it indicates a place of study, a college, or a university.

Tantriks evolved five symbols to represent what Western occultism calls the five elements.[10]

During a day of 21600 breaths, symbol of Macrocosm-Microcosm, a particular element may be more powerful than any other, as we saw with dark and light in chapter one. Just as the power of an element waxes, so too it wanes, and the next element in the sequence becomes influential.

Every time-bound thing is composed of these five elements, whether the 'thing' is dead or alive. Thus a living human body and a corpse are both composed of the five elements. It is only when the Divine Triangle of awake-awareness enters into the Thing that it becomes animated or alive.

This is a basis for our five flowering arrows of AMOOKOS, which

Esquires and Handmaidens

you will recall from the Pentagram Rite of the First Degree. The arrows are the five senses, composed of the five elements. An arrow symbolizes force going outward, the flowery arrow represents an Inner and an Outer movement. When the Triangle or Awake Awareness enters then the five Arrows or Senses flower. In the third degree the names and agencies of these five Great Goddesses or Maha Shaktis are revealed.

Work in the five Academies consists of ensuring that your senses or instruments or Shaktis are charged to the limit with the divine Shiva energy or Awake/Awareness. In other words, you must turn dry sticks into flowering blooms. The importance of these exercises cannot be overstressed. They form an indispensable foundation for your own City Of Shambhala or Maha Zonule.

The Microcosmic Mahazonule

To understand the purpose of the six month exercise it becomes necessary to introduce some further concepts. We consider Shiva-Shakti as ultimately inseparable, a unity. This is represented by the Bindu or point at the centre of a downward pointing triangle. Shiva is the Bindu of Awake-Awareness, Shakti is the triangle formed of Iccha (Will), Jnana (Knowledge) and Kriya (Action).

These three Shaktis together constitute the Triple Goddess, sometimes called Lalita (She Who Plays). These three symbolize the three Gunas or Primordial Threads or Qualities, from which is woven the Cosmos -Reconciling (Fire), Active (Sun) and Passive (Moon). By mutual blendings these three create the whole manifestation.

Maya - Goddess of Illusion

Because of the large number of possible blendings and reblendings, Awake Awareness (Shiva) may seem to become identified, conditioned, and confused. This illusion and delusion is called Maya - sometimes personified by a very alluring Goddess. She is also called Kanchuki Devi, that is, the Goddess of the Sheaths. These are five fold in number, so-called the five limitations.

    1 of Action (limited Kriya Shakti)
    2 of Knowledge (limited Jnana Shakti)
    3 by Desire (limited Iccha Shakti)
    4 by Time
    5 by Fate

Through the innumerable possible blendings and reblendings, the individual forgets she or he is Shakti-Shiva and considers herself or himself to be a limited individual (Purusha) with a certain nature

(Prakriti). This certain nature, a reflection or shadow or false image of Shakti, has a mental apparatus which is itself also a reflection of Iccha, Jnana and Kriya Shaktis.

For instance, the "I", or ego, or personal identity (Ahamkara) is the reflection of Iccha, and causes the Individual to think all that exists can be appropriated by him or herself - rather than Shiva-Shakti. Mind (Manas) is the main factor relating to association of thoughts, caused by the sense-impressions. The Intelligence (Buddhi) is that which understands the significance of external or internal sense-impressions.

The five elements are organized as a vehicle of Shiva-Shakti. They are animated by the triangle of Awake Awareness, with powers of action and powers of sensing.

The five powers of action are Excreting, Sexing, Grasping, Moving and Speaking. The five powers of Sensing are Smelling, Tasting, Seeing, Feeling and Hearing. By means of these ten instruments a human being is able to move in the world and sense the five impressions:

Scent Taste Sight Touch Sound
The five impressions which go round and round

These five impressions, in union with the three reflections of Iccha, Jnana and Kriya Shaktis constitute the Subtle Body, which may survive physical death.

At all times remember your unity with Shiva/Shakti. If you forget, or in our terminology are conditioned to forget this unity with Shiva/Shakti, the influx of sense impressions can create a new Maya or confusion. Thus ends the discussion on the thirty-six Tattvas of traditional Tantrika.

Practical Work

Experience shows that many people cease to be aware of their surroundings at an early age. The mental apparatus has a peculiar tendency to build up internal images, often randomly associated with other internal images, and compounded by word-descriptions. These in turn, act to prevent further sensing.

As an example, we have the word 'red' and most people would say that they understand what colour this word implies. Yet holding the concept of 'redness' can cause us to be unaware of the possible gradations. Our language is constructed in such a way that we usual ignore the shades of red. Our internal conception of many words can cause us to ignore the evidence of our senses. The map is not the territory.

A word can conjure up an internal image of the object it represents, yet the internal images may differ from every individual, and may be randomly associated with many other images and objects.

Esquires and Handmaidens

The curriculum which follows is intended to explore the limitations and conditionings which must be destroyed before further work can proceed. It is very important that you keep a separate and complete record of your twenty six weeks of sense experiment. The curriculum cannot end after twenty six weeks. The practice of Awake/Awareness is part of your continual growth.

The Daily Rite
There is an ancient rite or ritual which will daily assist you in this work. You must perform it upon awakening. No special preparations are necessary. Spend between five and ten minutes on it. Perform it while lying in bed, upon awakening.

With both feet together, visualize that a Flame of Great Effulgence which is the Fire at the End of Time, is kindled in the big toe of your left foot. Imagine this purifying Flame as striking upwards, enveloping your feet and legs up to the top of your head.

This fire is called Kalagni-Rudra, or Rudra (= Shiva = Adinath) as the Fire consuming all at the End of Time. It purifies by burning all into ashes, which themselves in our Adinatha line are considered sacred, and the only thing worth leaving when we exit this world of mortals. When all energies (Shaktis) cease to be then what is left?

Week 1 Differentiate as many shades of the colour grey as you can, always trying to remember if you have seen the same particular shade previously.

Week 2 In others' conversation listen carefully for the emotional content and note any discrepancies between the emotional content and literal meaning of the words the persons use.

Week 3 Be aware of the taste of all foods as they are eaten. Differentiate as many shades of taste as you can, and note preferences and dislikes.

Week 4 Utilize your sense of smell, firstly by trying to be aware of the fact you have a sense of smell.

Week 5 Maintain your awareness of the ground that you walk, sit and lie upon.

Week 6 Observe the facial features of others and your reaction to people who resemble others you may have known. What is the significance of various lines, wrinkles, tensions?

Week 7 Listen for sounds, particularly those emanating from the upper part of the sound spectrum.

Tantra Magick

Week 8 Take something you would not normally eat, and make yourself eat it regularly until it ceases to bother you. Completely switch your diet from what you usually eat during this week. Meditate on the significance of edible food.

Week 9 Distinguish various smell shades of one particular smell spectrum - flowers, people, etc.

Week 10 Distinguish various textures by touch of one particular class of things.

Week 11 Look for utility and design in any given thing. Why does any given thing have that particular shape? Move between the modifications of nature (artefacts) and nature Herself.

Week 12 Listen for vocal characteristics in people. Is any given voice soft, deep, whining, assertive, etc? What does the voice tell you about the inner being?

Week 13 How is the nature of an object changed by its setting?

Week 14 Listen for sounds emanating from the lower range of the audible spectrum.

Week 15 Feel your body. How does muscle tension affect the shape or tone of your body? Make a list in your diary. Look for tensions or lack of them in other people's bodies.

Week 16 Differentiate shades of blue. Record each occasion you discover a new shade, and where/when it occurred.

Week 17-20 Repeat the experiments in weeks one to four.

Weeks 21-25 Devise for each of these weeks an experiment based on Sight, Touch, Smell, Taste and Hearing respectively.

Week 26 Consolidate your twenty-five weeks using the date you have collected by deep thinking about the significance of the five senses, and any possible implications.

Esquires and Handmaidens

The Word 'Nâtha'

This is a sanskrit word which means Lord or Master, Lady or Mistress, depending on whether the 'a' at the end is short or long. It is a convention in our Order to omit the final 'a' and to spell it a simple Nath.

It implies that we are also as AMOOKOS members initiates of the ancient Nath Sampradaya or line of Oral Tradition. We bear this title proudly, as it is not an empty label.

Festivals and meetings

There are festivals of both Eastern and Western Traditions. The main ones are Spring Equinox (Air), Autumn Equinox (Water), Summer Solstice (Fire), Winter Solstice (Earth), Guru Purnima (Guru's Full Moon Day - generally falling in late July) (Spirit)

Footnotes

(1) *Tantrik Astrology* is published by Mandrake
(2) See page 69
(3) See page 51
(4) This may seem surprising to conventional astrologers but in our Tantrik astrology the square aspects are strong and highly significant, representing the four twilights.
(5) Bija mantras are the seed or essense of a deity in the form of sound.
(6) For more information on the Kleshas, or obstacle blocks to our goal of awake-awareness, see page 54
(7) This applies with equal force to the samples of ritual translated from Sanskrit into English
(8) Dattatreya Upanishad
(9) Avadhoot is one who has shaken off wordly feeling and obligation
(10) The Theosophical Society, inaugurated by Madam Blavatsky, and heavily influenced by Hinduism, incorporated wholesale much lore without really being aware of its significance. As a result the Theosophical Society published a book called *Nature's Finer Forces*, dealing with these so-called 5 Tattvas. Much of the information in this book was later adopted by the Hermetic Order of the Golden Dawn, and at 2nd or 3rd hand, became the basis for many of their experiments with skrying. The information contained in this paper is drawn from the original Tantrik sources.

The Third Grade - Craftswomen and Craftsmen

Symbolism of the Grade

Trowel:
Used in building our Lodge or Outer Temple of the Peacock Order. All our thoughts and deeds should be constructive and practical. It is you who has to develop our Craft for the good of all human beings. This cannot be done in a day. You will need to assemble all you require. This is adequate preparation. Then you will need to do the groundwork.

Gem:
Topaz.

Colour:
Yellow.

Lingam:
Clay. You must fashion this yourself.

Particular study:
Establishment of Zonule Buildings and artifacts of Will and Weirdglow. In this grade AMOOKOS members were asked to employ their craft to make an item useful to the Grand Lodge (Londinium Shambhala I).

Necklace:
12 beads, made of clay.

Zonule name:
Weird lodge

Animal:
White Horse. This is Kalki's vehicle.

Place of Meetings:
Work Rooms.

Tantra Magick

The Wanderer Delays a while to teach the Craftsmen and Women

The Ways of man who doubts and has not true Knowledge and Insight are always confused and lead him into bondage from which downfall must follow.

The masters are few but the slaves are many; only the Cosmic People can penetrate the mysteries to attain understanding of the world and space.

From sound Thought and Insight of the Spirit comes Dynamic Magick and in the Oracle of Changes we penetrate into our Cosmic Future.

There can be no dark without light and all things become meaningful by their opposites; even the stars are lit by the fuel of fantasy.

Obedience to the Cosmic Lord of Life is to live by understanding the Eternal Living Law of the Cosmos and its Eternal Contrast Change.

There are secret places of the mind and power is in the depths of one's own being but who will probe beyond the reach of sordid mundane life?

Thus the magicians use Change to free themselves from all worldly limitations for their real domain is the Boundless Joyful Cosmos.

Craftsmen and Craftswomen

Working the Grade

The Rite of Maha Zonule

Opening

Make a square of any suitable size and by any suitable means. In this rite nakedness is a prerequisite.

Eight bowls should be placed at the cardinal and midpoints (North, South, East, West and North-East, South-East, North-West and South-West). One extra bowl should be present within, full of pure water, together with a white flower and other accessories.

Sitting, facing the East, one should visualize in the East, then South, West, North, North-East, South-East, South-West, North-West a crystal Shambhala-Vajra of the purest effulgence, and with each one should say aloud or mentally *'Phat!'*

Say:

'I salute the line of Adinathas, and cast the circle of Semen's glow.
May this Island be Foursquare, and the Peace of Om dwell herein!'

Visualise yourself as a Shambhala Vajra. On your head place *Om*; on your genitals, place *Nam*; on your right hand place *O*; on your left hand place *Shiv*; on your right foot place *A*; on your left foot place *Ya*. Repeat three times.

Meditate in your heart on the Primordial Lord, Naked, White as Snow. Dazzling, with two arms and three eyes, both hands holding a diamond Shambhala Vajra, as seated on a white flower on an island of AMOOKOS, in the centre of an Ocean of Nectar, the Lord of Yoga Magick, the Master of Twilight Yoga, the Seed of Past-Present-Future, the Fourth, Knower-Knowledge-Known, the Adinatha.

In the four points of East, South, West and North are His Crystal Lingas of Rose Quartz, Ruby, Sapphire and Emerald. In the intermediate points are four heaps of the purest white ash. His Brightness is such that a Pillar of White Light extends from His Head to Heaven, and below, through the Island, to the Underworld.

Say:

I bow to that Meru Lingam in the Form of Consciousness, Lord and
Adinatha of AMOOKOS and the Naths.

Take a white flower, visualise Adinath in your breath, breathe onto the flower, place the flower on the surface of the water-nectar before you.

Say *Om Hamsa so aham*[1] and *I bow to Adinatha on the Island of AMOOKOS in the Centre of the Ocean of Nectar.*

Take a bowl in your right hand and pour Nectar into the empty

Tantra Magick

bowls in the order of East, South, West, North, South-East, South-West, North-West, North-East. Use all the liquid. Say *Om Hamsa* at every point.

This is the supreme rite of the Maha Zonule. At this point one may offer suitable enjoyment and substances to each of the eight points. If so doing, none should be neglected.

Other suitable Yoga Magick may then take place.

Closing

In the reverse order empty the contents of the eight bowls into the central bowl. Once again say:

Om Hamsa So Aham I bow to Adinatha.

Take the flower and breathe its essence back into your being. Meditate quietly for some little time.

The nectar in the bowl is holy water, and may be used as such. Alternatively, a little may be drunk, and the remainder poured at the root of a plant or a tree. Or one may bathe with it.

Notes

This Rite of Maha Zonule may, if preferred, be restricted to mental magick only. In such a case Adinatha becomes the Lord of Protective Magick, and may be meditated in this way if in any difficulty.

In such a case offering should be made of the five objects of the senses, food, breath, drink, sexual enjoyment, speech, thought, all.

Perform this Rite of Maha Zonule daily at best, or else weekly. In all cases it should be performed during a meeting of local Zonules.

The Magick of the Five Elements

Visualize the four quarters of your Zonule as follows:

Eastern Face: Presiding Goddess: a naked Woman seated in sexual union with a man. Her colour is yellow.

Southern Face: Presiding Goddess: a naked Woman seated on a Lion. Her colour is red.

Western Face: Presiding Goddess: a naked Woman seated on an Eagle. Her colour is blue.

Northern Face: Presiding Goddess: a Woman seated on a Bull. Her colour is green.

Upper or All Pervading Face: Presiding Devi, a Naked Woman situated on a Sphynx. Her colour is ultra-violet.

Subsidiary Shaktis

The Devi of each element has subsidiary Shaktis; these in turn have their

Craftsmen and Craftswomen

own subsidiary shaktis. In form they are like their presiding Shakti, and sit on a vehicle in a way similar to that Adi (primal) Shakti.

The Yantras of the Devi of each element are coloured yellow, red, blue, and green respectively - that is, they contain the colours of the presiding goddess, with their complementary colours.

Worship of the Door Goddesses - the Four Twilights

Air This Devi, with all Her subsidiary Shaktis, can be employed in magick for Knowledge. Her subsidiary Shaktis, 1, 2, 3, and 4 are the Shaktis of the Four Winds of the East, South, West and North. They

This is the Yantra to be used in the magick of the four Goddesses of the mundane elements:

	1	
4	5	2
	3	

The Yantra of Sphynx Devi

This is the shape of the Yantra for the presiding sphynx or Aether Goddess. It has 64 divisions and its colour is purple. These squares containing the Shaktis are the 64 hexagrams of the I Ching and the 64 Yoginis. Best still, this Yantra should be engraved on copper and gold, and wrapped in red cloth.

8	7	6	5	4	3	2	1
9	10	11	12	13	14	15	16
24	23	22	21	20	19	18	17
25	26	27	28	29	30	31	32
40	39	38	37	36	35	34	33
41	42	43	44	45	46	47	48
56	55	54	53	52	51	50	49
57	58	59	60	61	62	63	64

Tantra Magick

are Air of Air, Fire of Air, Water of Air, Earth of Air, and sit on a yellow, red, white and black man in turn. Their subsidiary Shaktis sit on members of the ape and monkey species. The Yantra should be engraved on gold.

Fire This Devi with all her Subsidiary Shaktis, can be worshipped for Subjugation or Attraction. 1,2,3, and 4 are Air of Fire, Fire of Fire, Water of Fire, Earth of Fire. She herself is Composite Fire. The subsidiary Shaktis are all similar to their Presiding Composite Devi, but sit on a Cheetah, a Tiger, a Leopard and a Panther respectively. The subsidiary Shaktis of these four sit on other male carnivores. The Yantra is to be engraved on copper.

Water This Devi with all her Subsidiary Shaktis, can be worshipped magickally for Peace, Fame, and Good Fortune. 1,2,3,4 are Air of Water, Fire of Water, Water of Water and Earth of Water. They cluster around their Presiding Goddess, and sit on a Hawk, a Falcon, a Sea Eagle and a Vulture. The subsidiary Devis of these Four sit on various kinds of fish, insects, amphibians and reptiles. The Yantra should be engraved on silver.

Earth This Devi, with all her Subsidiary Devis, may be worshipped for Stopping Things, Finding Hidden Treasure, Growth and Fertility. 1,2,3,4 are Air of Earth, Fire of Earth, Water of Earth and Earth of Earth. They are like their Leader, but seated on a Horse, a Goat, a Camel and a Buffalo. Their subsidiary forms sit on rodents, badgers, moles, weasels, etc. The Yantra should be engraved on lead.

The Composite Twilight - Sphynx Devi All Her Shaktis are Ultraviolet in colour, and for convention there are said to be sixty-four of them. They are of the nature of emanation and radiation, and can travel in the Air, on Earth, in Fire or in Water on their Beasts or Vehicles or Steeds which are like Sphynxes or Composite Creatures like Gryphons, Moebius, etc. They are called Lady Gamma, Lady Ion, Lady Charm and so on.

The female forms of all these Vehicles are the Yoginis themselves and may and must be treated with respect.

There are thousands of millions of other Shaktis, the nature of which depends on the proportions of the Five Elements.

The Rite of Protection - the Amulet or Armour of the Elements

Om! May Aether pervade my Being! May Air protect me in the East! May Fire protect me in the South! May Water protect me in

Craftsmen and Craftswomen

the West! May Earth protect me in the North!
May the Golden One with her hosts of subsidiary Shaktis shield me
in my thinking!

Air: Meditate on the Goddess of the East, suffused with golden light, very beautiful, of fair complexion, clothed in space, with three lines of turmeric smeared on Her forehead, surrounded by a halo like the rising sun, Her right hand indicating the giving of knowledge, Her left hand holding the Shambhala Vajra, wearing anklets, armlets, bracelets, and garlanded with yellow flowers, seated in sexual union with a man, a gentle breeze wafting Her hair, the embodiment of Air.

Say:
May the Green one, Surrounded by the Myriad of Mammals, protect my mouth and throat!

Earth: Meditate on the beautiful lady in the North, a lovely girl, clothed with space, wearing every kind of precious gem, garlanded with leaves, having anklets, armlets and bracelets studded with emeralds, in a vast pasture with beautiful trees, holding in Her right hand a sheaf of wheat, and in Her left hand an emerald Shambhala Vajra; seated on a powerful bull, the embodiment of Earth.

Say:
May the Wet one with her hoards of Fish, reptiles and Birds shield my abdomen!

Water: Meditate on the Goddess in the West, the beautiful maiden, clothed with space, eyes like deep pools, smeared with dust of turquoise gems, dripping with nectar, wearing armlets, bracelets, anklets all studded with sapphires, surrounded by a beautiful blue mist; holding in Her right hand a Chalice of Shambhala, and in Her left a sapphire Shambhala Vajra; seated on a beautiful male eagle, strong and keen eyed, the embodiment of Water.

Say:
And let Red fire and the Swarm of Carnivores guard my genitals always!

Fire: Meditate on the Goddess in the South, black hair, eyes like flame, clothed with space, smeared with red unguent, wearing a garland of red flowers and jewels and rubies, holding in Her right hand a flame, and with Her left hand holding a red Shambhala Vajra; seated on a magnificent and powerful lion, with mighty talons and teeth, surrounded by fires and flames, the heat of which burns up the world, the embodiment of Fire.

Say:
O Great Aether, Maha Shakti, with Your hundred million rays of all pervasiveness, be everywhere!

Tantra Magick

Aether: I meditate on the Queen of the Universe, all pervading, all encompassing, present everywhere, naked as space, studded with star sapphires, wearing a triple crown, surrounded by an intense purple light; showing the sign of giving with Her right hand, and holding in Her left and an amethyst Shambhala wheel, seated on a mighty sphynx called AMOOKOS Pyramidos [2]; with the head of a human being, the shoulders of a lion, the wings of an eagle and the haunch of a bull, composite creature of all the elements, mosaikos, the embodiment of Aether.

Say:
Let the Receivers of the Offerings guard me in the Intermediate points!
And may peace-freedom-happiness dwell within!

The Four Twilights

Times for each of the four Devis of the elements on a Solsticial Day

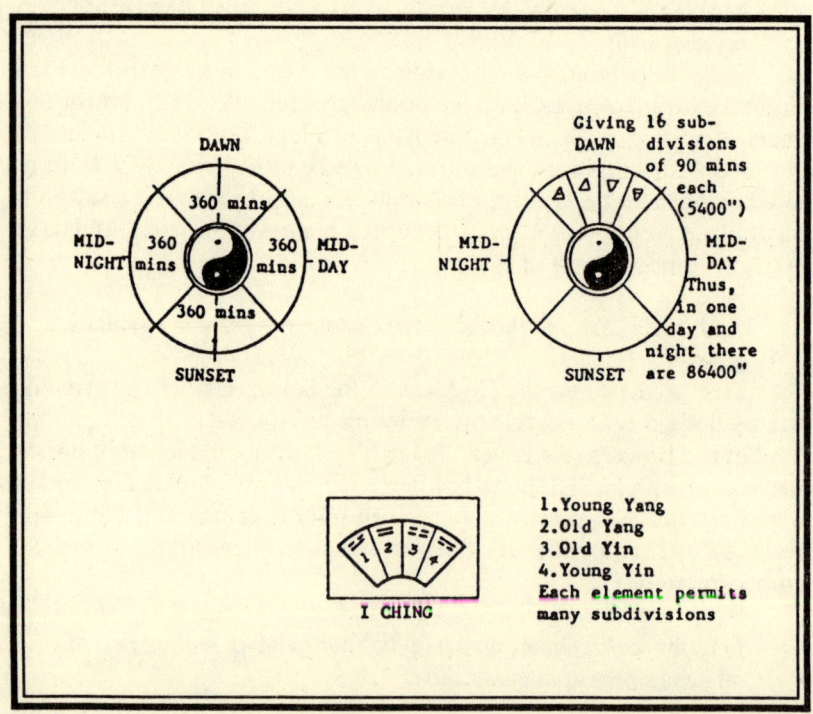

Craftsmen and Craftswomen

Each Devi rules six hours. In each of the four quarters Yang or Yin is on the increase or decrease. The four Elements rule ninety minutes in each period, the midpoints being Dawn, Midday and so on.

During other days of the year the calculation is made by drawing a time breath chart (horoscope) for dawn, and using the angles as your measuring stick for the right times of performance.

Let us express more clearly and precisely: a day and a night is a human being. The elements are in motion; they change.

Because a day and a human being are analogous we can learn much about both from studying each. Follow nature. There is one Cosmos! As shown in the diagram the I Ching can greatly help in an appreciation of these points.

Time-Breath Science

The alchemy of Adinatha - AMOOKOS the Shambhala or Azoth dissolving all.

Study pages 280-8 of "The Great Treatise" of *I Ching*.

Movement is followed by Inaction, Light is followed by Darkness. All complexity is based on this simplicity. Different movements of Yang and Yin, Shiva and Shakti, are taking place all the time. Nothing is fixed and all is movement. Yang and Yin move to Yin and Yang. One state cannot exist without another.

Our Solar system as a segment of the Infinity of Tao does not hide this fact. The diagram shows a model of the Solar system.

The apparent orb of Sun and Moon as viewed from earth is practically identical. However, even for us, Mercury, Venus, Mars and Jupiter seem to be Yang moving to Yin, the other four being Yin moving to Yang. The ridgepole occurs between Jupiter and Saturn.

These two bodies, for the conventional, are God and Satan. God - a benevolent old man.

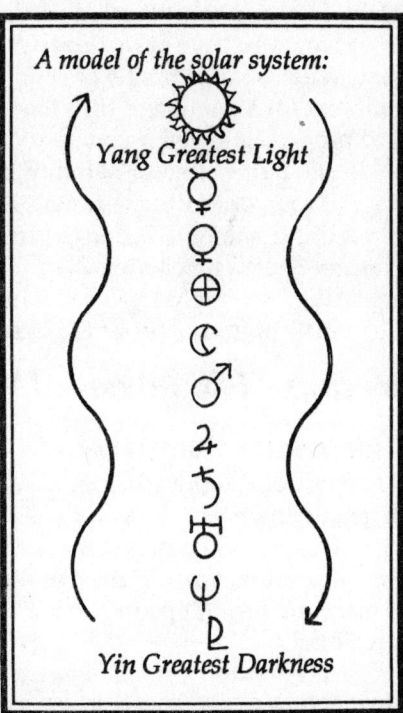

A model of the solar system:

Yang Greatest Light

Yin Greatest Darkness

Tantra Magick

Satan - a nasty old man. Do not allow the conventional interpretation to obscure the truth!

These Eight Planets have a definite sequence and importance to us, and in particular make their appearance in childhood development between conception and the age of four or five. This is their order:

Conception: The Void
Pluto - we learn to be alone in the womb
Cerebral
Mercury - we learn to think in twos (Mum and Child)
Jupiter - we learn to suck (assimilate)
Oral
Saturn - we learn to chew (scepticism)
Venus - we learn to give away (shit)
Anal
Uranus - we learn to control (don't shit)
Neptune - we learn to fantasize and dream
Genital
Mars - we learn to penetrate.

These Eight Great Powers can be seen as a developing ray from Maha-Shakti (our mother) towards genitality: the great light.

Now you have to work out for yourself how the model of the Solar system turns into a model of child development, and why the order is different for a woman or man than for Sol. (Note: you are learning fast and progressing well if your body is beginning to change).

The family tree of heredity is a Yantra of Life. Sun or Father is Rajas, Moon or Mother is Tamas, Earth is Sattvas. This is the growing plant of humanity. All things grow in the same way. We are part of Nature. She has Her own Plan. We can grow outwards and unconsciously (Pravritti Marg) or inwards and consciously (Nivritti Marg). The illustration shows our life like this tree.

Mantra - The Power of Words

The Mantra Hamsa

This part of the third degree deals with the mysteries of the mantra *Hamsa*, known variously as the Ajapa or Para-prasada mantra.

It is said to be the essence of *Om*.. Its efficacy is said to live in the fact that it is the form of the Absolute, Sun and Moon together, and it is a mantra which all people recite 21600 times every day through their breathing.

It is thus the form of time; as the Zodiakos has 21600 minutes, and

Craftsmen and Craftswomen

Amookos Awake-Awareness contrasted with the unconscious individual - how we differ

Asleep Pravrittamarg

Triply - nature flows in

The Being of the Five Elements

Manifoldly, actions flow out - words, work, children, a veritable thicket in which we forget ourselves - weeds gone to seed, grown in the world.

Awake Nivrittimarg

Triply - Great Nature Flows In

The being of the five elements. We sacrifice all earthly pleasures to the Divine and return to the Source.

The island of AMOOKOS - A Flower grows

is a complete circle, so macrocosm and microcosm have 21600 breaths, which is *Hamsa*.

It is a secret of the Nath-Kaulas that "Time is Breath".

Hamsa is said to be *Shabdabrahman* or the Absolute as sound.

Lord Shiva or Adinath is said to have five faces. Each mouth uttered mantras, tantras and yantras so that people could be freed from the ocean of samsara, or the wheel of time. Four of his faces are in the cardinal points and there is an upper face from which proceeded the Hamsa and all-pervading mantra.

The Hamsa or swan is said to be the vehicle of Brahma or the Absolute. Parahamsa is the name given to one who has attained to that, unknown to us, state beyond Hamsa.

Conception womb: darkness

birth : light

impressions ← *food*

↑ *breath*

centre is the fertile soil

Hamsa is the maintenance or inbetween state between Creation and Dissolution. Hamsa upholds the microcosm, which is also the macrocosmos.

The letter 'Sa' is Creation, and 'Ham' is Dissolution in the continuous breaths of a human being, this takes the form *HA-Sa-HA*. *HA-Sa* by rule of grammer becomes *HAMSa* or the Absolute's vehicle. *Sa+HA* by rule of grammer becomes *SO-AHAM* (Her or Shiva I am)

This continual sound of the Absolute is present within the heart of every man and every woman. Hamsa is said to be the Goddess Gayatri, seed of all Vedas.

However, within the mantra Hamsa is contained a very ancient Nath-science connected with the interplay in the human body between sun and moon. The breath is influenced by the various planets which are the rays or sheaths of sun and moon. When breath resorts to Hamsa, which is sun and moon conjoined, time stops and one is free of Kalachakra and Shiva-Shakti oneself .

The subject of Mantra cannot be divorced from the power of words generally. All words are made up of letters of the alphabet. In AMOOKOS the collectivity of these words is a Great Shakti or Female Energy.

Craftsmen and Craftswomen

Study of sound in the Academy of the Five Senses should have demonstrated to you beyond doubt that what people say is often not what they mean, or what you think them to mean. "Big" words like justice, peace, love inspire people to various activities, and you should always be aware that one word may mean very different things to different people. Because of this great hypnotic power we call this Goddess Maya.

Meditate on this point: *Can Association of Thought exist without words?*

A very well known phenomenon in hypnotism is the 'post hypnotic suggestion'. When someone is in the hypnotic trance it is suggested to them that on being awakened they will perform some or other act, often using a word by the hypnotist as a trigger. For example it may be suggested that on hearing the word 'moon' the person will stand up.

It has been noted that after people have carried out an action on a trigger word, if they are asked why they, in our example, stood up, they will give some very plausible reason. They may say "I stood up because I thought I saw someone I know out of the window" or "I felt as if I wanted to stretch my legs". It doesn't matter how many times they are 'triggered', they will always produce an excuse which may even make you doubt what you know.

This phenomenon is made use of by stage hypnotists, and the audience laugh at such stupidity. But the really laughable thing is that most people perform most actions in a state of hypnosis, and very often plausibly give 'reasons' which explain their actions. Ha Ha Ha.

The medium of hypnosis may be (1) words of others (2) emotions of others (3) unconscious imitation of others. The hypnotic subject is of a conditioned nature, a receptive and gullible robot whose whole being may contain nothing but other peoples' words.

As Adinaths we should made concerted attempts to test the truth of these statements above for ourselves, with an open mind, in ordinary life.

Yoginis of the Body Yantra

Here are the full meditations on the Yoginis of the Body Yantra. This develops the work in chapter two.

At Dawn: Meditate on yourself as one with Jnana Shakti
At Midday: Meditate on yourself as one with Iccha Shakti
At Sunset: Meditate on yourself as one with Kriya Shakti
At Midnight: Meditate on yourself as one with all three, Jnana Shakti as seated on white flowers in the region of your skull, Iccha Shakti on a red lotus in the region of your heart and Kriya Shakti on a lotus in

the region of your genitals.

Kriya Shakti - �

Meditate on the embodiment of Action, black as jet, naked, with beautiful rounded buttocks and high large breasts. Her anklets and bangles are made of silver and inlaid with sapphires. Her three beautiful large dark eyes are lined with coryllium. Her brow is smeared with purple unguent in the form of three lines; she is wearing two rings made of human bone.

Seated on the left thigh of Her Shiva and embracing him with Her right hand, like a Goddess of Love, holding his erect penis with Her left hand, She glistens with nectar, Her beautiful body quivering with love. Her neck garlanded with indigo-blue flowers, Her radiance and aura the colour of black effigence. Around Her and Her partner are corpses and skulls and both She and Her Shiva are smeared with the ashes from the cremation ground.

Jnana Shakti - ☾

Meditate on the embodiment of Knowledge as having a beautiful face and three eyes, and a crescent moon on Her forehead. She is of the whiteness of pure crystal or snow, or as white as cow's milk, and wears around Her neck a beautiful necklace of pearls which resemble a shower of nectar on Her beautiful high breasts, and Her ornaments are made from the purest crystal.

Her beautiful hair is braided and surrounded by a silver circlet, Her earrings are made of silver and each is inset with a beautiful pearl; Her body is graceful and slender, droplets of water shower Her form. She looks with love on her Shiva, touching His siddhi-staff with Her hand and holding him to Her with Her right hand, Her whole being shaking with emotion and Love. See them garlanded in pure white flowers, seated in a grove of lovely trees, and surrounded by white flowers, situated on an island in the middle of a lovely lake, the slight breeze gently agitating the tree under which they sit.

Understand that this tree is the letters of the alphabet. Its seed is Awake-Awareness, its roots are pure sound. Its branches, which are the letters of earth pervade the world; its leaves which are the letters of water shelter the three cosmoses; its buds, the letters of fire, ornament it like jewels; its flowers, the letters of air, make it beautiful and its fruits, which are aether letters, nourish all beings. Pure nectar drops from the branches of the tree onto the bodies of Jnana-Shakti and Her Shiva. This tree grows, fruits and flowers simultaneously throughout the year.

Craftsmen and Craftswomen

Iccha Shakti - ☉

Meditate on the embodiment of Free Independent Will, naked as space, golden red like ten million suns and ten million fires of dissolution. Her red form is shaking with sexual desire. After having bathed She has smeared Herself with red sandal paste and Her own menstrual blood. She has beautifully rounded hips and large breasts, Her restless eyes are lost in desire. After having embraced Her Shiva-love with Her right hand She had placed his penis within Her and is wet with lust. On each of Her beautiful arms are three red parallel lines. She wears gold earrings, gold anklets, armlets and bracelets. She is garlanded with red flowers and her hair is dishevelled. Her beautiful lips are slightly parted through her desire. Both She and Her partner sit on a beautiful red lotus, the stem of which has raised the flower to the surface of an ocean of blood.

Three Shaktis of Supreme Shiva

Iccha	Jnana	Kriya
Hrim	Shrim	Krim
Wake	Dream	Deep Sleep
Vame	Jyeshta	Raudri
Dameshvari	Varreshvari	Bhagmalini
Fire	Sun	Moon
Creation	Maintenance	Destruction
Rajas	Sattvas	Tamas
Lalita	Jvalamuhki	Kali
Knower	Knowledge	Object of Knowledge
Brahma	Vishnu	Rudra
Measurer	Measuring Stick	Thing to be Measured
Red	White	Black

Iccha Shakti's four Shaktis :- Pita, Malini, Harina, Rakta
Jnana Shakti's four Shaktis:- Dawn, Midnight, Dusk, Midday
Kriya Shakti's four Shaktis:- Nila, Asita, Karbura, Aruna
The meaning of the names of the eight Yoginis are: Pita = Yellow, Malinidevi = Flowergirl, Harinadevi = Green, Raktadevi = Red, Nilashakti = Indigo, Asitadevi = Black, Karburadevi = Grey, Arunashakti = Magenta See the Body Yantra, chapter two.

Tantra Magick

Parameshvari, Maha Aether, Great Spirit

Ultima-Shakti, in union with Ultima-Shiva has the above fifteen Kula[5]-girls as Her limbs - Iccha, Jnana and Kriya Shaktis, with their respective four Shaktis. Her limbs are the five elements combined with the three gunas in different proportions.

It is possible to meditate on these limbs as being Kali's digits (waning moon) or Lalita's digits (waxing moon) or as Jvalamukhi's unified digits. Each moon or Kula has its own fifteen digits and is itself Consciousness digit, the sixteenth.

It is also possible to meditate on these fifteen limbs as partaking of the nature of the five elements. Here are their traditional magickal colours and powers:

Purple - Driving away
Red   - Subjugation
White - Knowledge, fame, good fortune
Yellow - Paralysis
Green - Protection

If meditated on as the fifteen limbs of each of the three major shaktis of Adinatha they cause:

Red   - attraction
White - liberation, peace
Black - death

Inner Magick of the Body Yantra

Your work in the second degree will have familiarized you with the exteriorisation of the eight yoginis and their "worship" in a Yantra.

The Kaula view is, however, that inner magick is more potent than outer magick; that is, absorption is more potent than projection.

Now learn to interiorise the eight yoginis in the following way:

Visualise eight lotuses with their eight petals as being in the areas at the top of the head, brow, tongue, throat, lower abdomen, anus, base of genitals and clitoris/penis.

In the centre of each lotus visualise the particular yogini or shakti:

Start by meditating on the centre in the top of the head ending at the lotus at the clitoris/penis, then in reverse order start with the clitoris/penis and end at the head.

Spend five or ten minutes visualising these chakras as each radiating their own type of energy. Then visualise simultaneously the lotuses gradually dissolving into each other, so that Nilashakti dissolves into Pitadevi and Rakti-devi dissolves into Aruna-shakti simultaneously.

Craftsmen and Craftswomen

Then visualise Pita-devi and Aruna-shakti as simultaneously dissolving into Malini-Devi and Karbura-Shakti. Then visualise Malini-Devi and Karbura-Shakti simultaneously dissolving into Asita-shakti and Harina-Devi. Finally visualise Asita-Shakti and Harina-Devi dissolving into each other in the region of the heart.

Now visualise that from the union of these last two yoginis that the two centres of Moon and Sun have come into being. Visualise a Devi in the Moon centre and a Deva in the Sun Centre. Visualise that they are seated in a pleasant grove in the centre of the heart having sexual intercourse.

At the moment of their mutual orgasm visualise that the Sun and Moon are one and meditate on this bliss in your heart.

Now meditate upon the other centres emanating out of this love-bliss in the reverse order.

The Shri Yantra

The Shri Yantra is perhaps the most famous of all the Tantrika mandalas or magick circles. It is the diagrammatic form of the Goddess, considered as the Body or the Cosmos.

She is the Shakti of Time, or Kali. Her partner, with whom She is One, is Mahakala Adinath - Free from Time.

However, as the Shri Yantra is connected with the process of Creation, as this creation is primarily a sexual process, Kali is figured in the Shri Yantra symbolism as Lalita, the erotic or playful form.

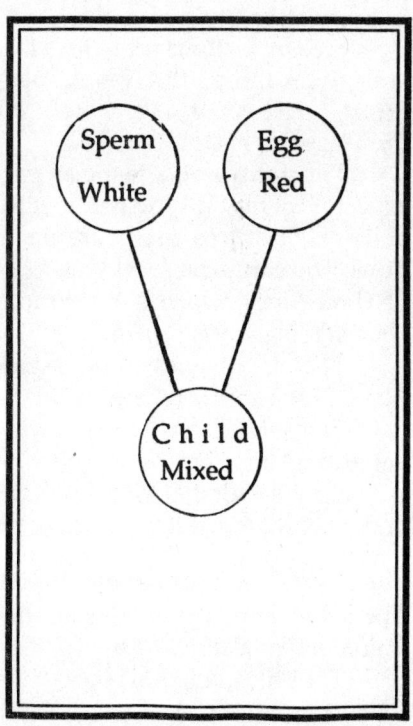

We learn from Nature that for creation to occur, the sperm of a man and the egg of a woman need to come together. This is known in Shri Vidya (Knowledge of the Shri Yantra) as *Kamakala*.

The Shri Yantra as a plant

We must take the Shri Yantra both as a plant and as a human body; both help us to understand aspects of its symbolism. It is not static, it is always in movement. If we take it as a separate thing it is only in order to understand this change, and not because it is a fixed symbol.

Two plants or People give rise to a third. Taken in isolation the Shri Yantra represents a human being, a Micro-Macrocosmos, the Body of Time. As Kali is Time and Manifestation, so too Adinath is sometimes figured as a corpse, or Witness of this Manifestation.

Lalita is also known as Tripura (three cities). These three cities are Her Shaktis or powers of Will - Knowledge - Action, and Creation - Maintenance - Destruction. They are also the three cities called Knower-Means of Knowledge-Known, or, as in our first degree, Measurer-Means of Measuring-Measured. But because each aspect is the Primordial Goddess, by meditating on the Symbolism of One Alone, it is possible to realise All.

The Seed of the Plant

The bindu is the point of Creation, Pure Sound itself, Immanent, about to outspread into the Shri Yantra.

The Stem of the Plant

This resolves itself into Moon, Sun and Fire. Moon is the five downward pointing triangles in the centre of the diagram, and fire the five upward pointing triangles.

Five times three triangles - the fifteen days of the lunar fortnight. Four times three - the twelve solar months of the year. Twelve plus fifteen - the twenty-seven letters of the AMOOKOS alphabet.

The Flowering of the Yantra

The eight petals and the sixteen petals together are the twenty-four aspects [6] of the Sun and Moon with the eight planets, but not with one another. The three circles are the three gunas encircling the Body of Time. The earthsquare with its four gateways is the Magick Enclosure of Three Lines, which is the world.

Human being or plant created

The plant passes on its essence through the seed, to form a new plant, Shri Yantra or Cosmos.

The Shri Chakra Yantra is within Time, that is to say it is a human being or a Microcosmos with all its Shaktis or Energies. (The Lord Shiva Adinath is beyond Time.) When the plant has flowered it is a human body. Before this it is in creation, or growth.

Shri Yantra as a Body

The Bindu, or point in the centre represents Shiva-Shakti Samarasa - the union of Shiva and Shakti.

The little triangle in the centre represents the Chalice of Shambhala,

Craftsmen and Craftswomen

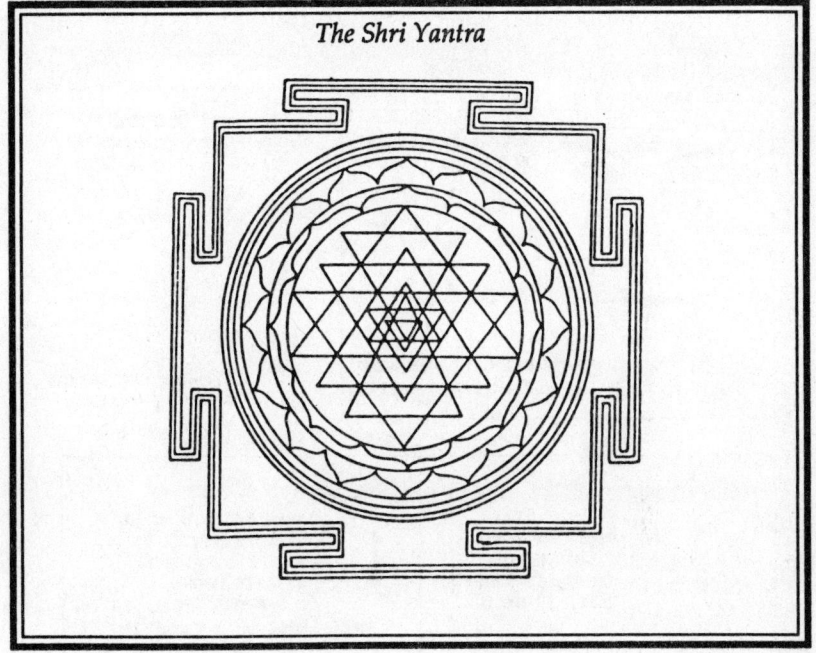

The Shri Yantra

or Moon, Sun and Fire, which are in the body as brain, heart or nerve plexus, and the grey matter in the spine.

The eight triangles represent the Knower or the Measurer, and is the City or Circle of the Knower.

The Two sets of circles each with ten triangles represent the means of knowledge and action, the five senses and the five ways of action together with the five impressions and the five elements. This is the City of the Means of Knowledge, or the Measuring Stick.

The circle with fourteen triangles represents the fourteen main currents of Psychic Energy in the Body, and thence all their extensions.

The eight petalled circle symbolises the sexual powers and attractions in the body, and the sixteen petalled circle symbolises the means of attraction.

The Earth square or Magick Enclosure is the physical body of the individual with its various elements.

There are thus nine circles of the complete Shri Yantra (Micro-Macrocosmos). In each circle Lalita exists in a triple form, presiding over the Shaktis or powers of each of the Circles. Each one must be taken as a combination or transmutation of Moon, Sun and Fire, the Chalice of Shambhala.

Here we have dealt with only two ways of looking at this Yantra,

Tantra Magick

VARIOUS YANTRAS OF THE WISH-FULFILLING TREE (HUMAN FRAME)

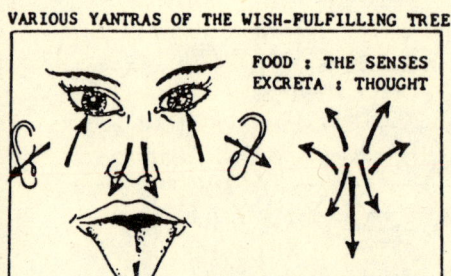

FOOD : THE SENSES
EXCRETA : THOUGHT

MAIN NADIS OF THE HEAD.
WE USE THESE IN MAGICK.

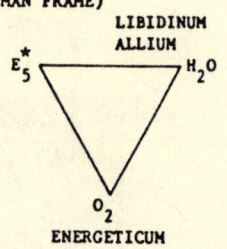

E_5^* — LIBIDINUM ALLIUM — H_2O

O_2 ENERGETICUM

*Element ESOTERIKOS
Atomic No 999

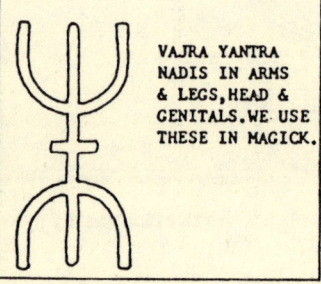

VAJRA YANTRA
NADIS IN ARMS
& LEGS, HEAD &
GENITALS. WE USE
THESE IN MAGICK.

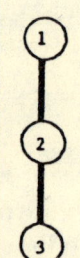

MERULINGAM. CENTRAL
NERVOUS SYSTEM IS A
NADI YANTRA.
1. BRAIN, MOON
2. NERVOUS SYSTEM AS THE
ROOT OF A RAMIFYING
TREE (SOLAR PLEXUS IS
THE CENTRAL POINT), SUN.
3. SPINE, FIRE

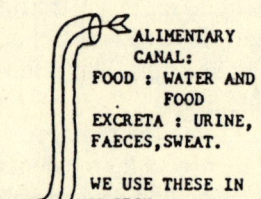

ALIMENTARY
CANAL:
FOOD : WATER AND
FOOD
EXCRETA : URINE,
FAECES, SWEAT.

WE USE THESE IN
MAGICK.

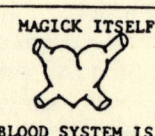

MAGICK ITSELF

BLOOD SYSTEM IS
THE ROOT OF A
RAMIFYING TREE.

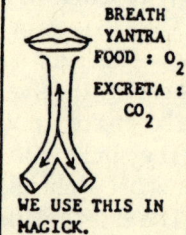

BREATH
YANTRA
FOOD : O_2
EXCRETA : CO_2

WE USE THIS IN
MAGICK.

WE USE THESE IN MAGICK.
BONE YANTRA, INTERLINKING WITH THE
HUMAN MULTICHORD.

Craftsmen and Craftswomen

in order to illustrate the depths contained within.

As the Father of our Earth the Sun may be taken as having twelve parts or Kalas which are Shares of Semen. The Moon as Mother may be taken as having fifteen parts or Kalas which are also Shares.

Because Shakti is the symbol of manifestation, we can take Her with Her fifteen Kalas or Eternities as one cosmos.

The Primordial Goddess is One, but with various aspects. Each aspect is called a Vidya or Type of Knowledge, and Her symbolism or Her Yantra tells us about the particular Aspect of Knowledge She enshrines.

We can take the primordial nameless Goddess as One Unity with Three Shaktis - these Three being Lalita, Kalika and Jvalamukhi. The last has twenty-seven flames or Jvalas, and is said to favour sadhus. She is Fire, Kalika is Moon and Lalita is Sun. Jvala is less known than Lalita or Kalika, but sits on a volcano and showers forth ashes.

Lalita herself is said to be of three forms - a Girl, a Mother and an Old Woman. These relate to the Power of Menstruation, to Creation, Maintenance and Destruction. We can see that the Erotic Form of Lalita has within Herself all elements, taken in a particular aspect or way.

The Fifteen Eternities of the Goddess of the Shri Yantra have names like lady of Sexual Desire, Yoni Adorned with Flowers, Lady of the Form of Fire, She who is always Wet, etc. Each of the mantras of these Devis are of an erotic nature, in consonance with the Presiding Goddess of the Circle.

Smashing the Five Kleshas

Cutting the tanglewood thicket

The second degree papers gave a brief outline of the tanglewood called five ob-blocks. You should have had some time to meditate on these and their possible ramifications in your being. This section of our wisdom teachings gives some techniques which may be of practical use. Record your results for yourself in your magick diary.

Ego Ob-block:

View yourself as an objective manifestation. Instead of thinking, feeling, sensing "I, John Smith, am doing such and such", think "the tangle of energies John Smith is doing such and such". Look at yourself as you perform actions. Observe all your behaviour as if it were another person performing the action.

Divide yourself as the tangle Jane Smith into Intellect, Feelings,

Tantra Magick

Bodily Experiences. Extinguish these three. See what is left. What are you without your three Shaktis?

Attachment Ob-Block:

Give away a prized possession to someone else. Do this so that your action will have useful repercussions not for you but for the other person alone.

Repulsion Ob-Block

View yourself as a social animal, as comfortable and accustomed to moving in fixed social circles. Get to know and understand people whom you would not normally involve yourself with.

Involve yourself in an activity that you usually try to avoid such as physical exercise for its own sake or household chores or a mathematical problem or writing a poem.

Clinging to Life Ob-Block

Meditate on this: The thing that I call "Me, Myself, I", is in fact a tangle of feelings, ideas and desires generated by prevailing circumstances and cosmic influences. This "I" is nothing more than a piece of driftwood to cling to and call my own, then what remains when I die? Surely if there is something of ourselves that is immortal it cannot be this.

Ignorance Ob-Block

Meditate on this: If "I" am so mistaken as to identify "Myself" with such partial aspects of the universe and call them "I" or "mine" then how can I claim knowledge of any other sphere or thing. How can I hope to see the wood in the midst of such a dense and tangled thicket?

Techniques for klesha-smashing using astrological theatre

The stage for this theatre is everyday life. The other actors are unconscious.

Act One - Mars and Neptune.

The sexual roleplay. Passivus is opposed and attracted by Activus. The technique is to assume either Mars or Neptune and observe how other people's Mars or Neptune reacts with yours. You have to make your act thoroughgoing and this implies that you are familiar with speech, voice pattern and muscle tone of the body. This is how Mars and Neptune function in relation to women and men.

MEN	WOMEN
HERO	SISTER
BROTHER	PRINCESS

Craftsmen and Craftswomen

This should be helpful to you. The following notes on Mars/hero is derived from the post Reichians. They would be horrified if they know the basis for their science is occult knowledge. Use the data to "assume the god-forms". The physical aspect of this is most important. Combine this with information from *Tantrik Astrology*.

Mars Hero

Self confident, outspoken but yet on guard. Eyes lively and open, jaw set and determined. Respiration abdominal. Vigorous. Desire to succeed strong. Quick and lively, full of drive. Obsessive. Always seems ready for action. Small narrow body structure. Genital activity strong. Eyes angry if failure seems possible. Cruel and hot tempered. Appears hard. View women as sexual objects for conquest, men as brothers.

Mars Sister

Adolescent quality about body. Body straight and lean with narrow hips, slender waist, normal shoulders, petite, tomboyish. Voice sharp. Decisive. Muscles with good tone. Appears hard. Views men as brothers, women as romantic heroes.

Neptune Princess

Suggestive. Irrational emotional outbursts. Chaotic behaviour. Dramatization. Waiting to be captured yet afraid of being caught. Obvious sexually based behaviour in combination with a specific kind of bodily agility. Lower part of pelvis soft and yielding. Upper part rigid and holding. Genital rigidities. Hysterical. Back rigid and unbending. Neck tight, head held erect in an attitude of pride. Front of body hard - chest and abdomen rigid; "unconsciously" seek situations which excite them, use of eyes, sexually submissive. Tease-resist-submit. View men as romantic heroes, women as sisters.

Neptune Brother

Shoulders held high. Forehead held high. Brotherly attitude to women. Look and act is if they have been frustrated. Never say no. Never say yes. Feeble. View women as sisters, men as romantic heroes (for this reason they are interested in sport or in any domain where hero worship is involved).

If you are female assume Mars/Sister and Neptune/Princess; if you are male assume Mars/Hero and Neptune/Brother.

Take each planet on a weekly basis. Try to familiarize yourself with it. Try to be it during the day and in contact with other people. If you have one of these planets powerfully situated in your birth-chart then still assuming the planet you should strive to see how your unconscious assumption of this planet affects others (the same applies to the follow-

ing two planets).
Act Two - Venus and Uranus

```
MEN              WOMEN
PLAYBOY  \  /  PROSTITUTE
FATHER    ><   MOTHER
```

Venus Playboy
Very interested in appearance and clothes. Soft spoken but vain. Cunning. Appears friendly with all, but given to secretly spiteful acts. Can't say no. Spendthrift. Views women as mothers.

Venus Prostitute
Lovely appearance, good looking, 'attractive' nature. Soft body tone. Seductive. Charm of eyes and manner as lethal as venus fly trap. Appears innocent and naive. Cannot say no. Lips sensuous with tendency to pout. Voice soft and well modulated. Eyes limpid. Views men as fathers.

Uranus Father
Father to wife. Tyrant to children. Ambition either power, money authority, control. Sadistic. A disciplinarian or a fascist or business man. Obstinate. Orderly. Parsimonious. Productivity the goal. Compulsive. Sex only a biological tension to be relieved. Everything reduced to objects. Often bald. Large bony frame. Heavy musculature. Solid jaw. Shoulders broad, buttocks tightly contracted. Inflexible and cold. A solid citizen. View women as daughters (to be looked after).

Uranus Mother
Mother martyr type. Mature behaviour. Awkward physical appearance. Lack of bodily grace. Self denial. Focused on role of mother. Fussy and urge to be always doing things for others. Views men as small boys.

We have dealt here in some detail with four planets and their manifestation in people. The implications of too powerful planetary influences are clear - they result in narrowness of being and expression.

You should find practice of astro theatre very helpful in both understanding yourself and the spirit fettered expression of others.

The Theory of Astrological Theatre

We have dealt with the four planets which have some striking characteristics. What distinguishes the group Venus, Uranus, Neptune and Mars from Pluto, Mercury, Jupiter and Saturn is that the former are sexually based and the planets Venus-Uranus-Neptune-Mars function in a sexual and interactive way within the pairs. Why?

Craftsmen and Craftswomen

A reason may be found in the order of the planets from the sun outwards excluding earth, which is

As contrasted with the known planetary pairs. We know that this order is:

But if you examine the first list again you will see the planets in the order:

How does the model for the planets work in a human organism. To understand this we will employ Gurdjieff's Enneagram - a very useful device in understanding octaves and patterns of growth and decay.

Place the planets on the enneagram as in the second diagram, and we have an explanation for both the Tamasic and Rajasic outward expressions of the planets Pluto, Neptune, Uranus and Saturn (on the left side) belonging to darkness. Mercury, Venus, Mars and Jupiter belong to light.

The pairs arise as follows: Pluto-Mercury and Jupiter Saturn adhere together as pairs. Neptune, Uranus, Mars and Venus and their interplay are represented by:

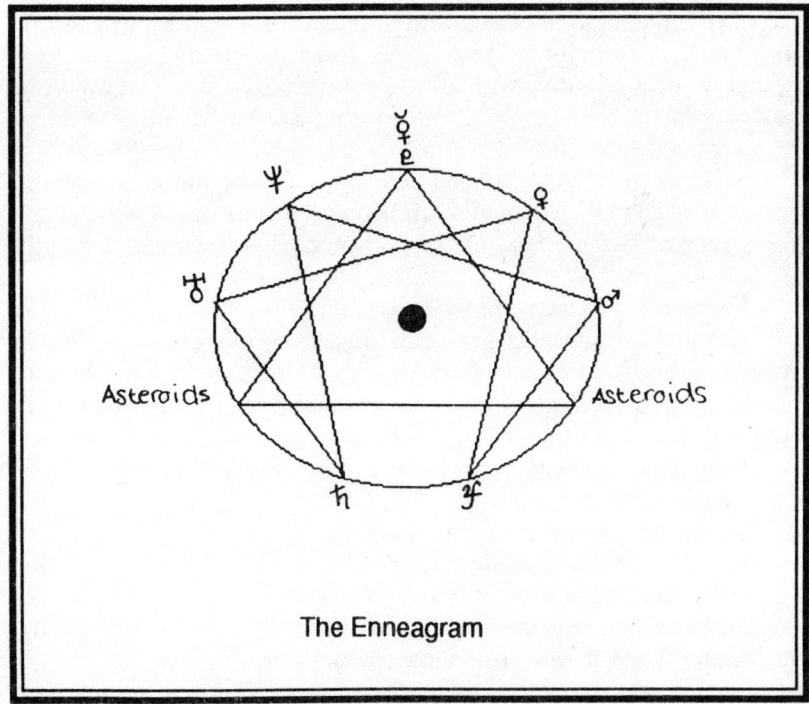

The Enneagram

Tantra Magick

We can understand this better by realising that Neptune and Mars and Venus and Uranus cannot exist except by a sexual process of mutual crossover. The breath armours of the individual planets show us the following:

```
soft  ♆ ⟍   ⟋ ♀  soft
          ╳
hard  ♅ ⟋   ⟍ ♂  Hard
```

Soft and soft do not go together, and neither do hard and hard.

Of course the yoni must be soft and the penis hard for this interplay to come about. The moon is soft and the sun is hard.

The Great Treatise in the I Ching confirms the astrological and the AMOOKOS view that an octave both expands and contracts within itself. As any plant grows (we take plant as a synonym for organism) a mutual process of backwards and forwards lines of time if proceeding. This enables us to produce the forward-backward enneagram shown in the diagram. You will need time to assimilate these ideas. Examine the diagrams and explanations carefully, meditating on them where necessary.

The Smashing of Conditioning

Accept your feelings (emotional and physical). Allow them to penetrate your head. Surrender to your head, heart and body - these often function independently, with disastrous results. Do not allow your head to crush your heart. Do not allow your head to ignore your body.

Knots

Many occur at the junctions in the Shri Yantra (human Body) - at the neck and genitals. You may find chronic tensions which prevent one brain or region of the body from feeling another. A great deal of energy is involved here.

Symptoms of Success (but not success itself)

Hot tingling sensations in neck muscles. Feeling of numbness in areas of the body, perhaps in face, legs, arms. Increased spontaneously easy breathing. Feelings of anger and frustration. Spontaneous body movements.

Resolutions or mantras to help carry things through:
I accept my emotions
I accept my physical senses
Meditate on the following Mantra:
Hrim - Red, in your genitals, Creation
Shrim - Gold, in your heart, Maintenance
Krim - Black, in your brain, destruction.

Craftsmen and Craftswomen

Parameshvari - your whole being
Svaha - as sacrifice
(whole circle = Parameshvari)
Or:
Om Hrim Shrim Krim (Dattatreya)
Parameshvari (His Shakti)
Svaha (In Sexual Union)

Life Force is energy

You can regard life-force energy as a quantity. If you have unconsciously tense armour much of this energy will be bound up in muscles, leaving little for other process to work in your body. The more tense you are, and the more obstacles, the less 'alive' you feel.

Conditioning

Imitation of parents and others on a subliminal level is frequently the root of conditioning, as we discussed under 'Mantra'. If you experiment with this you may notice, for example, that one word or gesture will swiftly reverberate around a room. This is the basis for much hypnosis. Conditioning moves from the intellectual to the physical level very swiftly. Once structured in muscles the psychic knot is 'forgotten'.

The 'Awakened' state is often taken by occultists to refer only to some nebulous transcendental realm. This most certainly is not our view. We mean it on an ordinary level - in the here and now.

The Ridgepole

This expression of the I Ching reveals the dynamic Magick of AMOOKOS. The Ridgepole is the fluid yet equipoised point existing between the two states of active/passive. The head is 'heaven', the Earth is at the feet. If you cause and help yang to extend too much it turns into its opposite. This is also true of yin. Upon this remarkable knowledge of the ancients depends much of the AMOOKOS lore.

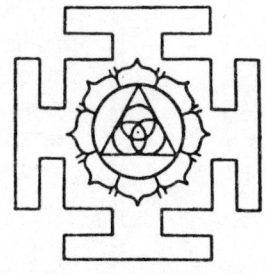

Tantra Magick

Two exercises to bring in more oxygen

These positions are drawn from the Chinese art of Tai Chi. As exercises alone they are useless. A certain mental attitude is essential. You should make the resolution to feel your body as part of each exercise. More particularly the exercises should bring you down to earth (with a bang if you're lucky).

Figure i

The feet are placed 15 to 18 inches apart with the toes pointing slightly inwards and the knees fully flexed. Contact should be maintained between the whole of the foot and the ground throughout the exercise. The hands are placed as in the figure and the whole body should arch evenly. It is important when doing this exercise to breathe fully and deeply. You may find that as it progresses you experience tingling sensations in the extremities of your hands and feet, and you may also find that your legs begin to vibrate. You should maintain this position as long as possible, and certainly longer than is comfortable, before adopting the second position (fig ii).

Fig i

Figure ii

With the feet in the same position and the knees still flexed, bend forward, tucking the head in and with your arms outstretched lightly touching the floor for balance. This position will invariably cause the legs to vibrate and you will probably become aware of the tensions produced in the calf muscles and hamstrings. Deep and full breathing should be maintained. To wind up this exercise you should straighten yourself up very gradually, straightening your head and shoulders last of all. These two positions comprise a single exercise.

Craftsmen and Craftswomen

Figure iii
This position is described fully by the picture. Again you should try to breathe deeply and fully throughout. This exercise is particularly good for loosening the band of muscles across the chest and the diaphragm.

Fig ii

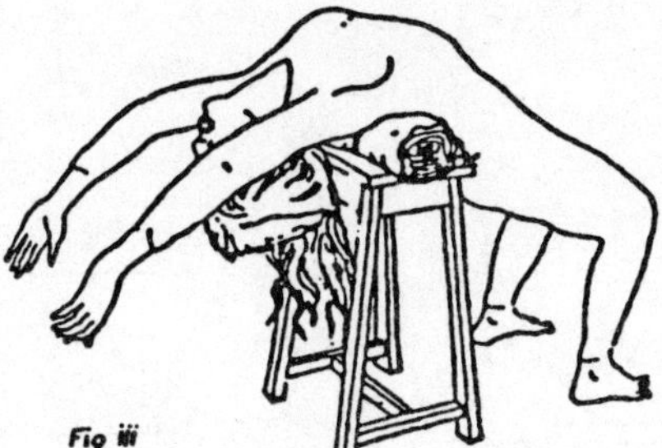

Fig iii

Tantra Magick

Protection Rite of Lord Datta (Dattatreya)

Meditate on the image below which is appropriate; meditate upon yourself as being one with Dattatreya or Dattatreya's Shakti. This may be done when one feels in need of great protection, or at the beginning of other magickal rites.

Meditation image for Dattatreya's Shakti: As a naked Sadhvini, smeared with red powder, with three red lines on forehead, arms and breasts, seated in meditation under the audumber tree, wearing a garland of red flowers seated in the umbra zonule in front of a slowly burning dhuni; surrounded on four sides by four fierce black dogs who face outwards towards the four cardinal points, wrathful and alert.

Meditation image for Dattatreya: As a naked Sadhu, smeared in ashes, with three white lines on forehead, arms and chest; seated in meditation under the audumber tree; wearing a necklace of rudraksha seeds; seated in the umbra zonule in front of a slowly burning dhuni; surrounded on four sides by four fierce black dogs who face outwards towards the four cardinal points, wrathful and alert.

You should offer your raw kleshas or ob-blocks to the dogs and to the dhuni to feed them. To extend the dogs from yourself, you should visualise that a ray of light extends to each of the four directions and then coalesces into the shape of a dog. At the end of the visualisation dissolve each back into white light and reabsorb them back into yourself.

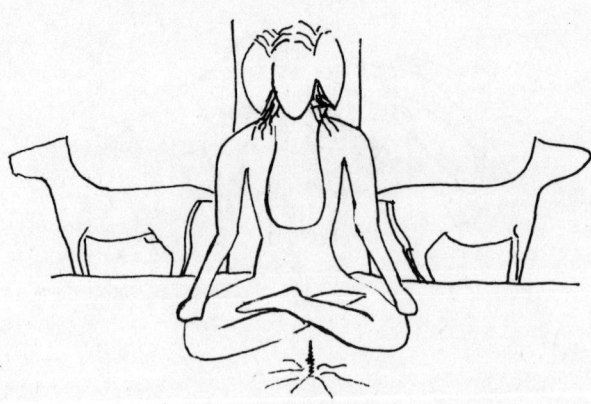

Craftsmen and Craftswomen

Study of Symbolism - Ganesha

In these papers we cannot stress enough that what is known as "Hinduism" is degenerated esoteric or occult lore. Such which has passed into the hands of the orthodox as been twisted out of context and has lost its meaning. But in the symbolism or iconography much of real occult value can still be discerned by the awake-aware.

As an example, in this section, we will discuss the hidden symbolism of the well-known God known as Ganapati or Ganesha. In present-day Hinduism Ganesha has degenerated into a God stopping obstacles, and His image can often be seen in shops. The shopkeepers 'worship' Him for the success of their trade.

If we look at a contemporary image of Ganesha, the iconography has preserved much of the occult or esoteric side, although the exoteric side has triumphed. We see a strange composite of elephant and man, and at the bottom of the picture a mouse or rat.

This is a glyph of the three worlds - of heaven, earth and the underworld, or sun, moon and fire. But in a very clever and wise way the symbolism has been drawn from the animal or mammal kingdom. In this picture man is the mean between the large or macrocosm and small or microcosmos.

Because of this triple symbolism Ganesha is connected with three gunas. His association with 'obstacles' comes from the great strength of the elephant, the intelligence of the human and the subtlety or ability to penetrate small spaces of the mouse or rat.

Ganesha is usually shown with four arms - these represent the four directions of space or the four elements - the God being the spirit or quintessence of these. This is also an indication of how the four turn into three and the three into one.

Ganesha means Lord of Hosts. As is usual in the Tantrik symbolism the Name is really an adjective. This adjective is also applied to Shiva. The Hosts are the hosts of spirits or denizens of the three worlds.

Although Ganesh is usually thought of as the son of Shiva and Parvati, the more cosmic view is that He is, simply, a specialised aspect or symbol of the primordial God. Because we follow nature, it is entirely natural that Primordial Godhead is represented by the penis, while the Goddess is shown by the yoni.

Knowledgeble about the creation of a child, the ancients, knowing of macro and microcosmos, found it natural to conceive of the sexual union of a woman and man as analogous to the creation of the cosmos.

You will not be surprised to learn that there formerly existed an esoteric group of Ganesha worshipers who worshipped the Ganesha Lingam and his Shakti as creators of our cosmos.

Contemporary images of the elephant-headed God invariably show Him clothed. Formerly this was not the case. We can note the following prescriptions for images drawn from a medieval and occult Indian work:-

Ganesha: Vermillion colour, three eyes with a large belly. In His four hands he holds a tusk, a noose, a goad and grants boons. He holds in His trunk a pomegranate and a crescent moon is on his forehead. He is adorned with huge serpents.

The symbolism relating Ganesh as being a child of Shiva and Parvati also has meaning. Their other son is Skanda or Kartikeya. He rides a peacock. If we take Shiva as guru, His sons, one with him in spiritual lineage, are the Divine and the Heroic dispositions. Ganesha and Skanda are princes and Shiva is the king.

The Ganesha Upanishad

We would ask you to examine this in the light that it is a resume of occult or magickal lore. Think about it with an open mind and analyse it for what it is.

We do not, in these papers, wish to restrict ourselves to the occultism of the Indian subcontinent. The gods and goddesses of many places and traditions can reveal a wealth of material which can expand our understanding. Occult symbols or sages can often preserve a whole body of wisdom and yoga magick. Some of this has been corrupted or garbled through the course of time by the ignorant. But the wise can reconstruct the past into the present for projection into the future.

Ganapati Upanishad

Auspiciousness to those who hear - thus the Shanti.
1 Om Lam I bow to Ganapati.
2 You clearly are the tattva. You alone are the Creator. You alone

Craftsmen and Craftswomen

are the Maintainer. You alone are the Destroyer. Of all this you certainly are Brahma. You plainly are the Essence.

3 Always I speak amrita. The truth I speak.

4 Protect me. Protect the speakers. Protect the hearers. Protect the givers. Protect the holders. Protect the disciple that repeats. Protect that in the East. Protect that in the South. Protect that in the West. Protect that in the North. Protect that above. Protect that below. Everywhere protect! Protect me everywhere!

5. You are speech. You are consciousness. You are Bliss. You are Brahma. You are Being-Consciousness-Bliss. You are the Non-Dual. You are plainly Brahma. You are knowledge. You are Intelligence.

6 You create all this world. You maintain all this world. All this world is seen in you. You are Earth, Water, Air, Fire, Aether. You are beyond the four measures of speech. You are beyond the three Gunas. You are beyond the three bodies. You are beyond the three times. You are always situated in the Muladhara. You are the Being of the three Shaktis. You are always meditated on by Yogins. You are Brahma, You are Vishnu, You are Rudra, You are Agni, You are Vayu, You are the Sun, You are the Moon, You are Brahma, Bhur-Bhuvah-Svar.

7 'Ga' the first syllable, after that the first letter, beyond that 'm', then the half-moon all together. Joined with 'Om', this is the mantra form.

8 Letter Ga the first form, letter a the middle form, m the last form. Bindu the higher form, Nada the joining together, Samhita the junction. This is the vidya of Lord Ganesha.

9 Ganaka is the seer, Nricad-Gayatri the metre, Sri Mahaganapati the God. "Om Ganapataye Namah."

10 Let us think of the one-toothed, let us meditate on the crooked trunk, may that tusk direct us.

11 One tusk, for arms, carrying noose and goad, with His hands dispelling fear and granting boons, with a mouse as His banner.

12 Red, with a big belly, with ears like winnowing baskets, wearing red, with limbs smeared with red scent, truly worshipped with red flowers.

13 To the devoted a merciful Deva, the Maker of the World, the Prime Cause, who at the beginning of creation was greater than nature and man.

14 He who always meditates thus is a yogin above yogins.

15 Hail to the Lord of Vows, hail to Ganapati, hail to the First Lord,

hail unto you, to the Big-bellied, One-Tusked, Obstacle-Destroyer, the Son of Shiva, to the Boon-Giver, hail, hail!

16 He who studies this Atharva Shira moves towards Brahma. He is always blissful. He is not bound by any obstacles. He is liberated from the five greater and the five lesser sins. Evening meditation destroys the unmeritorious actions of the night. At both evening and morning he is liberated from the bad and he attains Dharma-Artha-Kama and Moksha.

17 This Artharva Shira should not be given to those not pupils. If from delusion a person so gives, he is a bad person.

18 He who wants something may accomplish it by 1000 recitations of this. He who sprinkles Ganapati with this becomes eloquent. He who recites this on a 4th day becomes a knower of Vidya. This an Artharva saying "He who moves towards Brahma Vidha is never afraid." He who worships with fried grains becomes famous and becomes intelligent. He who worships with sweet-meat (modaka) gains the desired fruit. He who worships with samit and ghee by him all is attained, all is gained by him. He who makes eight Brahmanas understand this becomes like the sun's rays. In a solar eclipse, in a great river, or in front of an image having recited (this) he gets accomplished in the mantra. He becomes liberated from great obstacles. He is freed from great misfortunes.

Dream Power

Our view is that Wake Dream Deep sleep are one continuum called the 4th. Many problems arise because of mutual interpenetration. A daydream is an example of this, as is performing a whole series of complex actions without being aware of any of them.

In our dreams, wake state can exist. Usually we recall fragments the next morning when we awake. These fragments may contain hints of previous day's activities, of things which have happened when we were dream-awake, (mad association) or deepsleep - awake.

If you are interested in working with these fragments, the books of Dr Ann Faraday may prove useful to you. But it is possible to get bogged down in the world of 'Dream Power' or the mad pursuit of lucid dreams.

Members should carry out their own experiments with dreams and states of consciousness. As there are many levels to this work, and it is best carried out on a personal basis, we have not included it as a

Craftsmen and Craftswomen

formal part of the curriculum. But you are strongly recommended to incorporate elements into your own work.

A Tantrik View of Consciousness

People commonly experience three states: Being awake (Jagrat), dreaming (Svapna), and deep sleep (Sushupti). But the fourth state, Awake Awareness (Turiya) is not usually considered by ordinary science.

All of these states interpenetrate each other. A daydream is Svapna in Jagrat. A lucid dream is Jagrat in Svapna. Other subdivisions exist, and can be explored. One of the aims of AMOOKOS is to give members experience of the fourth state in each of the other three states.

Dream Record

Keep a separate diary by your bed. Use a biro or pencil to record dreams. Include the date, time, and the place of the record. Note your dreams first thing in the morning, immediately on wakening. At first you may find this hard to do, and there will be days when you record nothing, but persevere. Note fragments of dreams, however bizarre and apparently unconnected. Meditate on your dreams in the umbra zonule.

Dreams as a guide to Conditioning

Dream content often contains references to the previous day's events. These may show inner reactions to people, events, and even health. They are a great guide to discovering conditioning. The key to dream symbolism is often conundrum, ambiguity, and puns. This inner code is unique for everyone.

Senoi Tribe

This group of people incorporated dreams into their world-view. In the morning, family members shared their dreams. If someone met a hostile entity in a dream, she or he had to subdue it, and force it to give a dream gift to bring back into everyday life. The gift had to be something useful or aesthetically pleasing. The Senois seemed to regard hostile dream elements as split off parts of their own selves. Attempt this technique with your own dreams. Resist the temptation to interpret dream characters as being "outside" yourself. Dream friends should be cultivated. Dream animals like lions and tigers might represent latent powers. Before sleeping, ask for a specific dream on a specific point -- perhaps some split or confusion you've been unable to resolve in either the umbra zonule or in ordinary life. The tantrik goddess of dreams is Svapnavati Devi (She who goes in sleep).

Lucid Dreaming

Lucid dreams can be triggered mechanically by biofeedback methods. Alternatively, you can use symbols to trigger a lucid dream. Select a symbol which you decide will wake you up during a dream, for example simple yantras set in jewellery, a vajra, or any other such mnemonic.

Astrology and Dreams

Yavanacharya (Pythagoras) held that dreams were influenced by different planets affecting or transitting a birth chart. This is a fertile field for investigation. But you will need to keep a dream record for some time before you can start experimenting.

Daydreams

This is Svapna in Jagrat. The four states interpenetrate. A daydream is association of thought in a an apparently random manner. Try and keep records of these as well.

Siddhis - magickal powers : an inner view

Astral Projection, the idea that human beings have a subtle body attached to the physical one is very ancient and common to many different cultures.

Astral Projection and the body's Nadis

This is work of the Nadi Chakra. The nadis in the body are the conduits of vital energy or prana. There is a shakti called Pranashakti. Her Yantra is the nadi network in the body. Before being able to withdraw these nadis it is necessary to be aware of Pranashakti within your own body. These manifest as currents which can very definitely be felt physically. Their action hinges on breath being 21600 (ie the number of breaths in one day and one night).

The radiance or luminosity of Pranashakti extends a few inches beyond the body. Pranashakti is one with Nada (Sound in itself). When she is withdrawn, at first one's outer extremities become cold. One may feel slight breezes seeming to move over your limbs. Then the body becomes or feels as if it is paralysed. As Pranashakti merges with Nada Shakti a feeling of vibration commences until a stage is reached where this involving Pranashakti becomes sound. At this stage Nasikashakti may manifest.

This Nasika is a zig-zag phenomenon accompanied by strong emotional and physical feelings and perhaps inner sound moving from one side of the back to the other. This is often confused with so-called Kundalini - but recall that this term is loosely and incorrectly used by the uninitiated.

When all Prana has withdrawn into Nada, exit is made via the crown of the head. This process described in full here is exactly analogous to the death process. It is not easy to become proficient in this method, and indeed if you have equilibriated your three shaktis within

Craftsmen and Craftswomen

your body it is even harder. Remember it is only possible to withdraw Pranashakti when you are fully aware of how to extend Her - in other words, when you have experienced or had sexual intercourse with Her.

The difficulty with attempting astral projection before one has stabilized one's nadi web is that the withdrawn energy can cross into areas which have not been stabilised.

An old Shaivite tradition gives a clue to a sound occult basis for the different 'bodies'.

BINDU	BLISS"BODY"	SOUND IN ITSELF
NADA	KNOWLEDGE"BODY"	THE 4TH
MOON	IMPRESSION"BODY"	BRAIN
SUN	BREATH"BODY"	HEART
FIRE	FOOD"BODY"	GENITALS

A mantra and a human body have these components. Although these five elements are shown 'above' each other, the truth is that they are omni-pervading. How to realise in oneself Nada or sound in itself, this is enigma. The axis for the three centres of Moon, Sun and Fire, is Bindu, its axis is Nada.

The Astral Body is taken as the old idea of a body attached to the physical form by a thin cord is the breath body. It has duration in time, that is to say that it lives and dies. Only human beings and animals have one. Dead people, that is to say those whose core is rotten, don't.

DURATION	BINDU	SPACE-TIME OVULE
DURATION	NADU	DEEP SPACE
DURATION	MOON	MOON
DURATION	SUN	SOL (ENTRANCE TO DEEP SPACE)
DURATION 21600	FIRE	SPHERE OF YOUR BODY, IE THIS PLANET AND PLANETS

Other Siddhis

In the natural course of magickal self-realisation, of contact with your Guardian Spirit it is likely that powers will develop of their own accord. You should not make the mistake of regarding these as goals. Unless you are a steady thing yourself, no siddhis accrue.

They come naturally with spiritual growth, when you are relaxed, awake, and aware.

Only a few are mentioned below. They are mentioned here so that you will recognise them for what they are, they were all traditional powers of tantrik lore:

Remember the key to these 27 doors is: Sahaja-Samarasa-Svecch-acarya - equipose, spontaneity, the doing of one's true Will:

Tantra Magick

1 Sphere of three times (knowing past, present and future)
2 Penetration into words (understanding of language)
3 Penetration of previous rebirths (do not seek this, it may come of itself)
4 Telepathy (brain to brain contact. When this happens, it is a very great thing, and is not by any means linked to the world of ideas or thoughts)
5 Invisibility (this can be very useful)
6 Penetration into death processes (useful for our own passage)
7 Full Triple Being (ability to think-feel-sense as one)
8 Having Totalismus-Entire (strong as a lion, penetrating as a mouse, etc)
9 Penetrating into hidden things
10 Knowledge of Heaven
11 Knowledge of the Planets (time breath science, lower grade)
12 Knowledge of the Constellations (time-breath science, medium grade)
13 Knowledge of physical body and true medicine
14 Freedom from hunger and thirst
15 Great steadiness
16 Insight into the spirit worlds
17 Divine intuition (pratibha, you may be born with this but it is rarely a spontaneous manifestation)
18 Knowledge of consciousness
19 Power of the five-fold academy
20 Subtle body travel (it is easier to fly Pan-Am, do not in any way confuse this with creative imagination à la Golden Dawn)
21 Great Strength
22 Effulgence and radiance (this is aura, charisma, brightness)
23 Conquest of nature (you are nature)
24 Knowledge of time (You are time. Time-Breath science, highest grade)
25 Knowledge of all things
26 Recognition of intrinsic signs (the patterns of earth-bonded things)
27 Wealth

If you are involved in the occult for any length of time you will meet various people who claim one or more of these powers. Treat such claims with scepticism. Each siddhi is a very great thing and much rarer than most people would have you believe. Achievement implies a level of being of greatness.

Abandon the idea that every one is capable of progressing in matters of yoga magick. The current idea is that in our social-democratic societies anyone is capable of achieving anything they wish. But devoid

Craftsmen and Craftswomen

of will as 98% of people are, this can only be a delusion.

Food (our physical body) can be well or badly cooked. Quality varies from cook to cook. Being is the cohesive elixir which we are looking for. Devoid of spiritual being, people are mere beasts (pashus) and less than animals, which are at least true to their own natures.

Another point useful to remember is that you will know for yourself your own powers, but others will not (and indeed cannot) usually recognise them, other than by reacting to you in different ways, but usually unconsciously.

Do not neglect the fact that you have a wealth of so-called ordinary power which is mostly unused. People have reservoirs of potential which often stagnates because they do not have the three powers of Will-Knowledge-Action. The mantra here is 'carry things through'. Repeat this 108 times or your magick will be dust. Sometimes you may lose the thread but if you are sincere you will find it again.

A magician may not employ harm to another unless she or he has consulted two others of fifth degree or above. In rites of protection remember that you belong to a line which has existed for a very long span of time and that you may draw water from the well. Read Hexagram 50, cornucopia is our hidden name.

Tantra Magick

Time Lore

Rite of the three shaktis of 21600

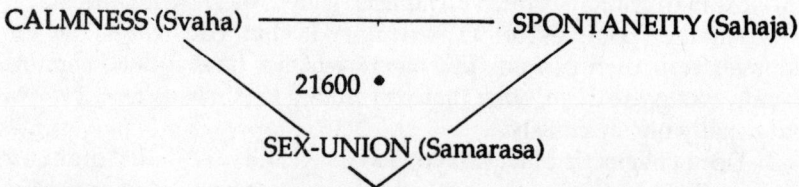

These are three specialised attendants of the Great Shakti of Time. They give whatever one desires, if all three are worshipped.
1 Right half of body male, left half female. In her-his right hand a Moon, in her-his left hand also a Moon.
2 In her right hand she holds a set square, in her left hand a compass.
3 In her right she holds a Sun, in her left hand a Moon.

Time Tantra

Purification or infusion of any substance
1 To prepare a powder, water or substance infused with any of the powers (shaktis) of Time, you should face the appropriate direction, choose the right time, and draw (using the breath method) the appropriate shakti into whatever substance you are magically preparing.
2 If, and only if the direction is inimical, you should, beforehand, draw the Tortoise Yantra with its head facing the inimical direction and within an earthsquare, shown in the diagram.
(i) You should visualise the following form of Shiva in your heart:-
(ii) As black as coal, holding sword, skull, trident and damaru.

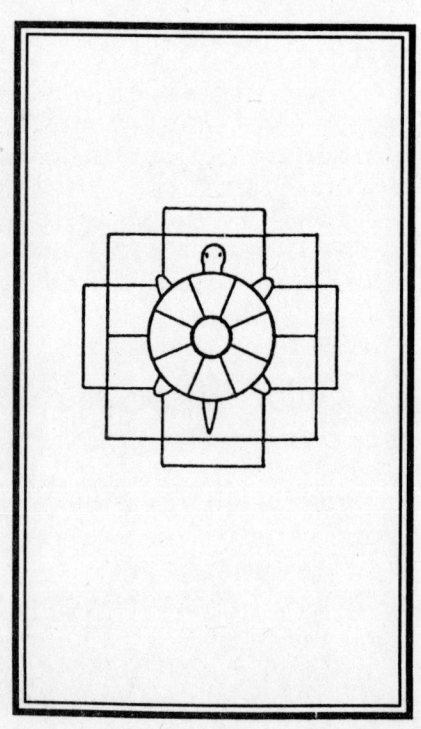

(iii) Then you should indraw Him into the Yantra above and offer incense, flame, water and food, then reciting the mantra 108 times:
KSHAM KSHIM KSHUM KSHAIM KSHAUM KSHAH
I WORSHIP THE LORD OF THE PLACE SUCH AND SUCH, PHAT!
After this worship, indraw the Lord of Place and proceed. Leave the Yantra where it stands for the duration of your magick.
3 To worship a Time Shakti you should visualise Her in your heart and offer mentally the five sense impressions before outdrawing Her.
4 After She has been invoked and duly worshipped, once again indraw Her by breath before ending the rite.
5 The mantra for each, which you have to recite at least 216 times is:-
OM HRIM SHRIM KRIM (Name of Shakti) SVAHA

Kali Kaula Kula Mahakala Akula - the Wheel of Time

Kali is said to be the presiding Goddess of the Naths. Her Guru line numbers amongst its members both Matsyendranath and Gorakhnath. She is the Shakti of Time. Time itself is Shri Mahakali, and Her spouse or alpha ovule is Shri Mahakala Bhairava, at once beyond and one with Time.

Time is viewed as terrible because its inexorable process consumes the cosmos. From Mahakali emerges a cluster of lesser Shaktis which are her Shaktis of Creation, Maintenance and Destruction. These are the yoginis and Door Protectors of the Body Yantra.

Sometimes shown at the centre of the Kali Yantra are five triangles, each point of which represents one of her most intimate forms known as Nityas, a word meaning 'eternity' or 'day'. These days are the waning digits of the Moon.

Kali, like many other great Vidyas, is a complete cosmos within Herself, and 'astrology' is the key to understanding Her symbolism. To become 'free from time' implies to be one with Shri Mahakala Bhairava, Adinatha, Alpha Ovule, Dattatreya, Mrityunjaya (Shiva as Conqueror of Death) etc, etc.

The *Kalachakra* is the wheel of time, or the Wheel of Kali and her subsidiary Shaktis. Her path is the path of Return. Return to what? To the orgasm which started our own particular planet or cosmos off, and which is Kali Kala Samarasa or the perfect assimilation within oneself of both Sun and Moon, symbolised by the eclipse.

Kaula A kaula is a Knower of Kali Kala.

Kula A Kula or Clan is a family or cluster of Kali's Shaktis, some of

wich build, some of which maintain, and some of which withdraw.
Akula Lack of Kula, that is to say, the Alpha Ovule.

Major Subdivisions of the Wheel of Time

Kali and Kala are symbolised by the Sun and Moon. Their sexual union symbolises that which unites them, ie their child or earth. Because this has the property of reconciling Kali and Kala it is linked to the Guna Sattva. Moon is Tamas and Sun is Rajas. All these factors are interchangeable.

Both Sun and Moon have four modes or Kulas which correspond to the four elements Earth, Air, Fire and Water. Earth too has four modes. In the case of the Sun the modes are known as Mercury, Jupiter, Venus and Mars. The Moon's Kulas are Pluto, Saturn, Uranus and Neptune. These are therefore subdivisions or Kulas or clusters of Shiva Shakti.

If we take each of these four as engaging in sexual intercourse they produce:

Shakti + Shiva = Child
Pluto + Mercury = Air
Saturn + Jupiter = Earth
Uranus + Venus = Water
Neptune + Mars = Fire
Moon + Sun = Aether

These are Kali's fifteen Nityas, and the digits (Kalas) of the waning moon: Full Moon (Sun), Mars, Fire, Neptune, Uranus, Water, Venus, Akasha, Saturn, Earth, Jupiter, Mercury, Air, Pluto, New Moon (Moon)

Mahakali is therefore unified time, or the collectivity of all Her Kulas or Yoginis. One is already liberated - the Alpha Ovule. The trick is to 'rearrange' the kulas so that (1) both time and its power becomes apparant to you and others according to one's Will, and (2) that one realises oneself as source and expression of Time.

Basis of Time

Number, that is to say the interplay of Shiva and Shakti, is the basis of Time. The whole circle of Zodiakos with the planets, sidereal constellations, angles and Navamshas is Mahakali Herself.

The lesser subdivisions of Time come into play as a result of the reblending of the lesser Kulas with the greater Kulas. In a time breath chart there are two great realms which are reconciled in a human being, taken as a symbol of Sun/Moon or Shiva/Shakti perfect assimilation:

Craftsmen and Craftswomen

Realm 1	Realm 2
Kala (Sun)	Kali (moon)
12 Kalas	15 Kalas

A microcosm is defined as the blending of the 12 Kalas of the Sun and the fifteen kalas of the Moon. Both sets of Kalas are again made up of the sexual union of Shiva and Shakti in various proportions. A microcosm is therefore sometimes called a 27, whereas a Macrocosm is a 108.

This mutual blending of the Sun and Moon or Shiva-Shakti is represented in the Shri Yantra in a unified way by the 5 downward pointing triangles (5x3), and four upward pointing triangles (4x3).

Time and its units

The basis of Time in Tantrika conception is breath. This is because it is the mean unit of the whole cosmos as food. In Ayurveda there is 'food' as food, 'food' as breath and 'food' as sense impressions. All three types are consumed at a different rate or vibration.

In one day and one night a balanced human being is said to breath 21600 times. 10800 are for the night and 10800 for the day. A day and a night is one breath for the Sun. One year is one day for the sun. A lunar fortnight is one breath for the Moon.

The basic unit for Zodiakos is also 21600 (minutes of arc). Of these 10800 are of Kala and 10800 or Kali. This divides Zodiakos into a Solar and a Lunar half. Within this Wheel of Time there are therefore six sidereal constellations which are Lunar, and six which are Solar. These two sets are each divided into a Solar and a Lunar half, and of these two sets of three are made up of a Rajasic (Solar), Tamasic (Lunar) and a reconciling component.

This gives the funadmental division of the constellations into 12 - the 12 Kalas of the Sun. They are in units of 4.

The Time Breath Chart

This individual chart shows how the particular blendings of the 27 solunar Kalas affect a being's breathing pattern.

Magickal application of the Time Breath Chart

A balanced human being breathes 21600 times in day and night. An unbalanced human breathes haphazardly according to the pattern found in the Time Breath Chart.

Tantra Magick

The 27 Hormonal Messengers or Dutis
The heart and core of the 27 Kalas is Samarasa beyond Time and Space, modified into 27 various blendings of Sun and Moon. This is the Supreme Hormone.

A Time Breath Chart shows a predisposition to one of more of the various hormone - Kalas. It is these which are both affected by and affect the breath, the physical apperance, the muscle structure, armourings and so forth.

The Kaula Circle
This was made of up 8, 15, or 27 Shaktis with their Shivas, selected according to the predispositions in their individual TBCs of the various Kalas, the conception being that by assembling these Dutis, Suvasinis or Nityas one created on earth a model fo Macrocosm.

Poison or Nectar
Whether these messengers act as poison or nectar depends on their individual positions in relation to the Wheel of Time at the time of birth.

Poisons
These are configurations which affect a human being on Sun, Moon and Fire levels to produce psychological disturbances structured in mind, feelings and muscles.

Planets as Symbols of the Hormone-Dutis
Because the planets or Yogins as a circle within themselves contain all the elements of the Micro-macrocosm, it is possible to take their effects as a measure of all other effects occuring in the wheel of time.

Nectar or Poison
If nectar, the planes give beneficial results to the individual in whose chart they are found. If poison, the planet gives detrimental effects. However the significant thing from the point of view of a Nath-Magician is that, whether 'good' or 'bad', the person manifesting them is partial.

Chief Nectar is Samarasa
The goal of the magician working with the Kala Chakra is the liberation within her or his being of the Maha Amrit or Super Nectar, which gives both access and birth to all other nectars.

Sama Consciousness
This is Equipoise, a state of being in which partial identification with one

Craftsmen and Craftswomen

or another thing cannot happen.

Kala Chakra Method of Magick
This involves the individual fight against particular identifications based on one's own Time Breath Chart and the seeking of Sahaja, Sama, Samarasa based on return to one's source and freedom from action-reaction shown in one's own chart.

Uncover the Moon!
The most vital magickal aspect of the action of these Kalas of the Moon is that they partake of Maya or seizure, and have power only when a magician is unconsious of them. Because they simultaneously affect the three levels it is impossible to attack their lawful results using one only of mind, body or feelings.

Observe others!
Because others unconsciously express the effects of the hormonal Shaktis, observation of them in others is the key to uncovering their effects in you. For example if you see 50 people with Pluto Kala strong and each manifests the same hormone or type, and if you yourself know that you have Pluto Kala strong it is reasonable to presume that you also may be unconsciously expressing Pluto Kala. This gives you a strong basis for working.

Shaktis themselves oppose Kalachakra Magick
Because the Kulas have as their function the covering or englamouring of their own Shiva consciousness they oppose the process.

Heroines and Heroes
You must be heroic if you venture far on this path of tantra as everything in you and much outside opposes the work. Therefore make a strong resolution to carry things through.

Yogas in Kalachakra
Any place where on Kala in a Time Breath Chart is connected with any other Kala or Kalas is a yoga or union of two hormonal factors.

Final Conclusion
Reread *Tantrik Astrology*. Reread the chapters on Time. If you have not already done the work of observation, now is the time to start. Start a separate Record and tabulate your results from people you chance across in real life.

Tantra Magick

The Kaula Upanishad

May the Kaulika triumph! May Varuni triumph! May Truth triumph! May fire triumph! May all living things triumph! Obeisance to the Absolute, Obeisance to Earth. Obeisance to Fire. Obeisance to Air. Obeisance to Guru! You are like the Cosmos! You are that, self-evidently! I will speak of the Divine Law. I will speak the truth! That must protect me! That source of speech must protect me! Protect me! Protect my speech! Om shanti shanti shanti.

Now the investigation into Dharma. (It is) knowledge and mind. It is the unified cause of both knowledge and liberation. Siddhi emanating from one's own being arises from liberation. The five objects of the senses constitute the expanded Cosmos. Of all this Knowledge is the Essence. Yoga is liberation.

The absolute without parts (Adharma) is the Creator. Ignorance is the same as knowledge. Ishvara, the Lord is the Cosmos. The eternal is the same as the transitory. Knowledge is identical with the absence of knowledge. Adharma is Dharma. This is liberation. The five bonds constitute the essence of real knowlege. The Pinda is the producer (of all). In that is liberation.

This is real knowlege. Of all the sense the eye is the chief. One should behave in a way opposite to that expected. One should not do this devoid of rightness. All this is the essence of Shambhavi.

The amnya not to be found in knowledge. Guru is oneness. All is oneness within the mind. Siddhi does not exist in unitiated ones. Abandon pride and so forth.

One should not reveal this. One should not discuss this with pashus. Even weak argument may contain the truth. One should not make distinctions. Do not speak of the secret of self. One may speak of it to a pupil.

Within a Shakta, outwardly a Shaiva, in the world a Vaishnava. This is the rule. Liberation comes from knowlege of self.

Condemn not others such as Adhyatmika. Do not perform vows. Do not establish oneself on restraint. Binding oneself is not liberation, a Kaula should not practice outwardly. One becomes equal to All. One becomes liberated.

One may read these sutras at sunrise. One attains the siddhi of knowledge. This is the knowledge of Self, or Parameshvari.

May the Kaula triumph!

Om shanti shanti shanti.

The Kaula Upanishad is complete.

Symbols used in this Book

PLUTO	♆ or ♇
MERCURY	☿
JUPITER	♃
SATURN	♄
VENUS	♀
URANUS	♅
NEPTUNE	♆
MARS	♂
SUN	☉
MOON	☽
EARTH	⊕
ARIES	♈
TAURUS	♉
GEMINI	♊
CANCER	♋
LEO	♌
VIRGO	♍
LIBRA	♎
SCORPIO	♏
SAGITTARIUS	♐
CAPRICORNUS	♑
AQUARIUS	♒
PISCES	♓
AETHER, SPIRIT	⊛
AIR	△
WATER	▽
EARTH	▽̶
FIRE	△

Appendices

Glossary Of Terms

AGNI
The fire God

AMRITA
Elixir of Immortality

AVADHOOT
One who has shaken off worldly feeling and obligation

AYURVEDA
"Science of Longevity", Medicine

AZOTH
"The star in the East", an alchemical fluid or solvent

BHAIRAVA
Terrifying aspect of Shiva. His right hand or southern face, whence the term right-hand path.

BHIKKU
Religious mendicant or Buddhist monk

BIJA MANTRA
Seed syllable of a mantra

BINDU
The point at the centre of a yantra

BRAHMA
The divine essence or spirit from which all created things emanate

CHAKRA
Centres of energy within animal psychic anatomy

DATTATREYA
Legendary guru of the Mahabharata and of the Naths, said to have three aspects

DEVI
Goddess

Tantra Magick

DHARMA
Cosmic Law or Duty

DUTI
Messenger

GUNA
"Quality", There are said to be three basic constituents of all matter viz: Sattvas, Rajas, Tamas

ISHVARA
Supreme being

JAGRAT
Awake

KALACHAKRA
Wheel of time, horoscope

KAULA
Member of a clan

KAMAKALA
Consort of the love god, essential syllable of a mantra

KLESHA
"Fetters", The five kleshas or obstacle blocks are Ignorance, Ego, Attraction, Revulsion and Clinging to Life.

KULA
Clan

KUM KUM
A red fungal pigment used to draw ritual marks on the body. Also turmeric

KUNDALINI
Feminine and serpentine energy said to rest at the base of the spine

LAMA
Tibetan Buddhist priest

Appendices

LALITA
"She who plays", wanton primal goddess whose divine play creates the phenomenal universe

LINGAM
Penis, real and symbolic

LOKAPALA
Guardian of the world or the points of the compass

MANTRA
"Instrument of Thought" a magical series of sounds capable of transforming consciousness and the world

MERU
The cosmic mountain at the centre of the micro and macrocosm

MODAKA
Sweetmeats suitable as sacred food for the gods

MOKSHA
Liberation

MULADHARA
The root centre of animal psychic anatomy. Its exact location is subject to much debate, but is said by most authorities to be located in the area between the anus and the genitals

NATH
"Lord, Sovereign or protector", name adopted by members of an ancient tantrik cult founded by Matsyendranath

PARAHAMSA
Highest guru, Shiva

PARAMPARA
The right to confer Tantrik initiation

PASHU
Beast, Man of Earth, one of three categorization of humanity commonly used in Tantra, the other two are Diva (God) and Vira (hero)

Tantra Magick

RUDRAKSHA
"Eye of Rudra": Rudra is an ancient name of Shiva. Rudraksha is a red bead made from a dried berry found only in Nepal. A magickal rosary usually has 108 rudraksha beads

SADHAKA
Tantrik Adept or magician. One who take the most direct or effective path to liberation

SADHU
One who take the most direct path to liberation, holy man or woman

SAMARASA
Equipoise, of bodily and mental humours

SAMPRADAYA
A particular line or tradition passed from guru to student

SAMSARA
The round of rebirth and death, the cycles of existence

SANNYASI
One who renounces all earthly concerns and is devoted to the pursuit of spiritual liberation.

SHABDAHBRAHMAN
The divine principle of sound that is the source of all phenomenal existence

SHAKTI
"Power", usually personified as the female consort of Shiva or other deities

SHAMBHALA
The cosmic city that is one of the objects of the Tantrik visualization. The legendary future birthplace of Kalki, the final incarnation.

SIDDHIS
The traditional magickal powers that are developed by the Tantrik adept

Appendices

SVECCHACHARA
"Doing ones own will" : One of the highest Tantrik ideals

TATTVA
"Thatness": One of the essential constituents of physical nature

UPANISHAD
"To sit near": Secret knowledge given to those that sit near the feet of the guru. A class of mystical writings that set at rest ignorance by revealing knowledge of the supreme spirit

VAJRA
"Thunderbolt", Tibetan: Dorje. A magickal weapon that combines elements of the dagger and wand

VAMA MARG
"The left current", perhaps derived from the left or northern face of Shiva. Usually applied to magickal tantra.

VEDA
"Knowledge", usually applied to the celebrated ancient text of Hindu religion, said to be the actual sounds of the divine as heard by the Vedic shamans. Four such Veda exist: Rig, Sama, Yajur and Atharva. The last of these is the most unorthodox and magickal

YANTRA
"Tool or devise", a generic term applied to mystical diagrams and models characteristically used in Tantra as the focus of mental magick.

Appendices

Index

A
ADHARMA 112
ADINATH 7,23,37,39,42,51,61,69,78,83,107
AGHARTI 29
AGHORA 55
AGNI 99
AJAPA 76
AKASHA 108
AKULA 108
ALCHEMY 39
ALPHA OVULE 9
AMRITA 99
ARMOUR 72
ARTHARVA VEDA 57
ARUNA SHAKTI 46,49,50,53,81,82
ASITA DEVI 47,49,50,53,81,83
ASTRAL BODY 103
ASTRAL TRAVEL 31
ASTROLOGY 26,39,107,111
AUDUMBER 57,96
AURA 33
AVADHOOT 57
AWAKE AWARENESS 58,61,77,80
AYURVEDA 42,109
AZOTH 75

B
BENARES 8
BHAIRAVA 37,58,107
BHIKKU 8
BHU 41
BINDU 23,41-2,45,59,84,103
BIO-ENERGY 33
BODY YANTRA 39,41-2,44-53,79,107
BRAHMA 7,57,58,81,99
BREATHS 58
BUDDHA 57
BUDDHI 60

C
CEYLON 8
CHARISMA 33
CHI 33
CHINA 11
CLAIRVOYANCE 32
CONSTELLATIONS 104
CROWLEY, ALEISTER 7

D
DADAJI 7,9
DATTA SEE DATTATREYA
DATTATREYA 7,37,57,93,96,107
DEVA 99
DHARMA 112
DHUNI 96
DIGAMBARA 57
DOG 96
DRAGON SEAT 17,23,41,44
DUTIS 110

E
ELEMENTS 47,58,70,75
EMOTIONS 92
ENNEAGRAM 91-2
EQUIPOISE 110

F
FOURTH 42-4

G
GANAPATI - SEE GANESH
GANESH 52,97
GAYATRI 78
GENITAL 25,76,103
GOLDEN DAWN 10,26,31
GORAKHNATH 7

Tantra Magick

GURDJIEFF 91
GUNA 7,39,58,97
GURU - SEE DADAJI

H
HAMSA 72,76-8
HARINA DEVI 46,49,50,53,81,83
HEAVEN 93
HORMONE 108
HOROSCOPE - SEE TIME BREATH CHART
HYPNOSIS 79

I
ICCHA (WILL) 40, 48,59
ICCHA SHAKTI 45, 59,79-80,82
I CHING 8,54,75,92,93
ICONOGRAPHY 97
IGNORANCE 54,88
INITIATION 18
INTERCOURSE 83
ISHVARA 112

J
JAGRAT 101
JNANA 40,48,59
JNANASHAKTI 45,59,79-80,82
JUPITER 46,50,75,76,91,108
JVALAMUKHI 81,82,87

K
KALA 87,107,108,109
KALACHAKRA 11,50,78,107,110
KALI 50,81,82,83,87,107,108,109
KALIKA 24,87
KALKI 28,67
KAMAKALA 83
KANCHUKI DEVI 59
KARBURADEVI 46,49,50,53,81,82

KARTIKEYA 52,98
KAULA 8,55,56,107
KLESHA 54,87,96
KNOT 92
KRIYA 40,48,59
KRIYA SHAKTI 45,59,79-80,82
KULA 82,107,111
KUM KUM 45
KUNDALINI 102

L
LALITA 50,59,81,82,83-4,85,87
LAMA 8
LINGAM 24
LOKAPALA 24,25,
LOKANATHA 7

M
MAHAKALA 83
MAHAKALI 107,108
MAHASHAKTI 76
MAHAZONULE 59
 RITE OF 69-70
MAHENDRANATH - SEE DADAJI
MALINIDEVI 46,49,50,53,81,83
MANAS (MIND) 60
MANTRA 41,47,51,71,76,78,92
MARS 46,49,50,53,75,76,88-90,91,108
MASONS 42
MAYA 37,59,79,111
MEDITATION 30
MERULINGAM 23,37,69,86
MERCURY 46,50-1
MNEMONICS 27,53
MODAKA 100
MOKSHA 100
MRITYUNJAYA 107
MULADHARA 99

Appendices

N
NADA 102,103
NADI 86
NASIKA 102
NASIKASHAKTI 82,102
NATH 7-12,39,44,56,57,63,107
NEPTUNE 46,50-1,76,88-90,91,108
NILASHAKTI 45,49,50,53,81
NITYAS 108
NIVRITTI 76,77

O
OCTAVE 91-2
OPAL 37
ORGASM 83

P
PARAMAHAMSA 78
PARAMESHVARI 82,93
PARAPRASADA 76
PARAMPARA 9
PARVATI 98
PASHU 11,54
PENTRAGRAM RITE 21,59
PHAT 19
PITADEVI 45,49,50,53,81,82
PLATO 58
PLUTO 45,50-1,76,91,108,111
POISON 110
PRAKRITI 60
PRANA 102
PRANASHAKTI 33,102
PRATIBHA 104
PRAVRITTI 76,77
PSYCHOKINESIS 32
PURUSHA 59
PYRAMID 25,74
PYTHAGORAS 26,102

R
RAJAS 39,76,81,91,109
RAKTADEVI 46,49,50,53,81,82
RUDRA 61,81,99
RUDRAKSHA 96

S
SADHU 7,57,96
SAHAJA 103,106,111
SAMA 110-1
SAMARASA 50,84,103,106,107,110,111
SAMPRADAYA 9,32,54
SAMSARA 7,78
SANNYASI 7
SATTVAS 39,76,81
SATURN 46,50-1,75,76,91,108
SENOI TRIBE 101
SHABDABRAHMAN 78
SHAKTI 24, 26, 39, 40, 48,51, 56, 61,75,83,93,110
SHAMBHALA 9,20,23-4,28-9,59,84,85
SHAMBHALA VAJRA 69,73
SHANTI 98
SHIVA 7, 24, 25, 26, 39, 52, 55, 58,61,75,78,97,100,106,110,111
SHIVA PARTICLE 39,41
SHIVA-SHAKTI 19,24,39,59-60,78,108
SHRI YANTRA 39,83-7,92,109
SHOSHITA 21
SIDDHIS 30,103-4,112
SIDEREAL 26,39
SKANDA 98
SKRYING 15,28
SPHYNX 25,70-1
STAFF 37
SURYA 52
SUSHUPTI 101
SVAHA 106
SVAPNA 101
SVAPNATIDEVI 101
SVECCHACARA 10,57,103

Tantra Magick

T
TAI CHI 94
TAMAS 39,76,81,91,109
TATTVA 98
TIME BREATH CHART 24,109,110-1
TIME BREATH SCIENCE 56
THEATRE (ASTROLOGICAL) 88-92
TIBET 8
TORTOISE 18,106
TRIPURA 84
TWILIGHTS 24-5,74
TURIYA 101

U
ULTRA-VIOLET 70
ULTIMA-SHAKTI 82
UMBRA ZONULE 17,21,25,28,30-1
UPANISHADS 57,98,112
URANUS 46,50-1,76,90,91,108

V
VAYU 99
VAJRA 23,86
VAMA MARG (LEFT HAND PATH) 29
VEDA 57,78
VENUS 46,50-1,75,76,90,91,108
VIDYA 87,100,107
VIRA 11
VISHNU 7,52,58,81,99

Y
YANG 75,83
YANTRA 23,48,78,86,102
YAVANACHARYA - SEE PYTHAGORAS
YIN 75,93
YOGA 7
YONI 24

Z
ZONULE 10,11-12,25,31,47

Modern Studies in Tantra Magick from Mandrake

Also in this series:
Michael Magee's *Tantrik Astrology*

This book builds on the unique astrological system introduced in *Tantra Magick*. Astrology radically different from the kind often seen in popular newspapers. Tantrik Astrology demonstrates that astrology is central to the process of deconditioning. It provides a basis from which an individual can release her or himself from the fixed breath patterns set by their birth chart or horoscope.

ISBN 1869928067(Mandrake 1989) $9.95/£4.95 128pp pbk

Available from:
good bookshops
or direct from the Publishers.
Send for free catalogue of tantrik and related books to PO Box 250, Oxford, OX1 1AP (UK)
or telephone
UK (0865) 243671